2,002
Ways to
Show
Your Kids
You Love
Them

2,002 Ways to Show Your Kids You Love Them

CYNDI HAYNES

Andrews McMeel Publishing

Kansas City

00 01 02 03 BIN 10 9 8 7 6 5 4 3 2 1

Library of Congress Cataloging-in-Publication Data
Haynes, Cyndi.
    2,002 ways to show your kids you love them /
Cyndi Haynes.
        p.   cm.
    ISBN 0-7407-0484-2 (pbk.)
    1. Parenting Miscellanea. 2. Parent and child
Miscellanea. 3. Love, Maternal Miscellanea. 4. Love,
Paternal Miscellanea. I. Title. II. Title: Two thousand two
ways to show your kids you love them. III. Title: Two
thousand and two ways to show your kids you love
them.
HQ755.8.H42 2000   99-40477
649'.1—dc21   CIP

Book design by Holly Camerlinck

───── Attention: Schools and Businesses ─────

Andrews McMeel books are available at quantity
discounts with bulk purchase for educational, business, or
sales promotional use. For information, please write to:
Special Sales Department, Andrews McMeel Publishing,
4520 Main Street, Kansas City, Missouri 64111.

Dear Reader,

Childhood passes in the blink of an eye and it is my most sincere wish that this book inspires you to make this magical time even more special by showing your children in lots of different ways just how very much you love them.

Most warmly,
Cyndi Haynes

For Andrew, whom I love more
than words can possibly say.
Thank you for all of the love
and laughter that you have
brought into my life.

———— ♥ ————

Loving a child doesn't mean giving in
to all his whims: to love him is to
bring out the best in him, to teach
him to love what is difficult.

Bruno Monsaingeon

———— ♥ ————

1. Host a regular family worship service in
   your home.

2. Watch the sunset together from different
   scenic spots all around town.

3. Serve your child breakfast in bed
   complete with
   * Yummy food   * Fresh flowers
   * Small, surprise gift * Morning comics

4. Always expect the best of your child.

5. Try to see the world through your child's eyes.

6. Unplug your television set for a
   * Day   * Week
   * Month   * Year

7. Teach your child the Golden Rule. Live by the Golden Rule.

8. Get a newspaper from the day your child was born and give it to him on an important birthday.

9. Create a time capsule for your child and bury it in the backyard.

10. Research your family tree together.

11. Play in the snow together. Try activities like
    * Making snow angels   * Sledding
    * Building snow forts   * Building snowmen
    * Making snow ice cream

12. Teach a new word to your child every day.

13. Have a low noise level in your home to create a peaceful environment.

14. Treat your child as you would your best friend.

15. Embrace the present moments with your child instead of wishing he was younger or older.

16. Refrain from doing two things at once. Give your child your full attention!

17. Remember that people are always more important than things.

18. Smile at your child many times throughout the day.

19. Tickle your child—gently please!

20. Instead of spending New Year's Eve at a big bash with your friends, stay at home with your child.

21. Become your child's biggest
    * Cheerleader   * Fan   * Coach
    * Mentor   * Champion

22. Send a card and sign it from "Secret Pal."

WAYS TO HAVE MORE TIME FOR YOUR CHILD

* Shop through the mail by using quality mail order catalogs
* Order your groceries on-line
* Get up a little earlier than normal
* Work at your most productive time
* Learn to say "no" to unnecessary commitments
* Delegate chores to others
* Make a list of what you need to do

---

23. Propose a milk toast to your child at dinner tonight.

24. Celebrate National Ice Cream Month with your child in July.

25. Serenade your child with songs from your heart.

26. Fix something fun and different for dinner tonight.

27. Teach your child to celebrate the gift of life.

28. Encourage your child to send money or gifts anonymously to a family in need.

29. Always fix a good breakfast for your child as it is the most important meal of the day.

30. Give your child a list of 10, 20, 50, or 100 ways that she has brought joy and happiness into your life.

31. Teach your child that ugly ducklings turn into beautiful swans.

32. Climb trees together.

33. Make homemade ice cream together.

34. Always give your child a second chance.

35. Remember that you are the parent, not the child. You are the adult. Be sure to act like one even under the most trying circumstances!

36. Explain to your child what you have learned from him.

37. Teach your child to respect his elders.

38. Act silly together.

39. Read fables that teach great truths.

40. Interview your child on tape and save these wonderful pieces of family history.

———————— ♥ ————————

Other things may change us, but
we start and end with the family.

"Bloodlines," Esquire

———————— ♥ ————————

41. Don't smoke.

42. Teach your child's Sunday school class.

43. Always keep your promises!

44. On family trips, take along
    * Games   * Puzzles
    * Toys   * Books
    These will help to entertain your child.

45. Tell your child the wonderful story about how you and his other parent met and fell in love.

46. Instead of lecturing your child, try
    * Illustrating   * Communicating
    * Quietly talking and sharing

47. If you are angry with your child, count to ten before you speak or act.

48. Imagine how big you look to a small child.

49. Buy fun souvenirs for your child while on vacation.

50. Send birthday cards to your child's closest friends.

51. Give your child a trophy for being a great kid.

52. Praise your child immediately when he does something right or does a good job.

53. Repeat secondhand compliments that you hear about your child to your child.

54. Use charts and graphs at family meetings to bring life to the discussions.

55. Always be on time for your child's events.

56. Encourage your child to
    * Invent   * Create   * Imagine
    * Dream   * Plan   * Discover
    Our world will be better for it!

57. Guide your child through life instead of pushing her through it.

58. Have your child join a kids' book club.

59. Keep in mind that tears are healing agents. When your child is sad, let the tears flow.

60. With your child, help out an elderly neighbor.

61. Love your child unconditionally.

62. Knock on your child's bedroom door before entering.

63. Teach your child that it is okay to be different from other kids. After all, some of the greatest among us have been quite unique.

64. Tell funny little stories about your daily life to make your child feel more connected to your world.

PARENTING AFFIRMATIONS

* I love being a parent and I cherish the
    role I play in my child's life.
* I gladly meet all of the responsibilities of
    being a mom/dad.
* I create a wonderful home environment
    for my family.
* I bring out the very best in my children.
* I give my child a positive self-esteem
    boost every day.

65. Be glad to see your child whenever she
    comes through the door.

66. Refrain from bringing up your child's past
    mistakes.

67. Always chaperone your child's parties when
    they take place in your home.

68. Ban soap opera viewing in your home.

69. Resist placing labels on your child.

70. Serve cold treats on hot days.

71. Take a small child to a petting zoo to help instill a love and respect for animals.

72. Let your children see you being kind and helpful to your parents.

73. Keep a humidifier in your child's room on nights that he is sick.

74. Give up caffeine as a family. You will all feel better for it.

75. Set up play dates with your child, no matter how old she is.

76. Get your child to school on time.

77. Be your child's knight in shining armor.

78. When you say "No," be sure that you mean it and stick to it.

79. Pray with your mate in front of your child.

80. Have a Frivolous Day once every six months.

81. Teach your child to finish what she starts.

82. Keep a diary expressing your love for your child and allow your child to see it.

83. Before your child gets too old to enjoy family vacations, take him to see
    * An ocean   * Mountains
    * A large city   * A small, quaint farm

PARENTING QUESTIONS TO ASK YOURSELF

* Am I teaching my child to be an optimist or pessimist by my example?
* Do I teach my child not to judge others?

---

84. Attend all of your child's recitals.

85. Learn CPR. You might need it to save your child's life someday!

86. Always go the extra mile for your child.

87. Buy a hammock for the backyard. You and your family will enjoy it enormously.

88. Have your child read The Book of Virtues by William J. Bennett.

89. Be courteous to your child at all times.

90. Wish upon a star together and share your dreams.

91. Turn your house into a home.

92. Put flannel sheets on your child's bed on cold winter nights.

93. Give your child a Steiff teddy bear no matter how old she is.

94. Learn to laugh at yourself in front of your child.

95. Breast-feed your baby for it is so good for her and for you.

96. Dance with your child in public.

97. Proudly display your child's picture on your desk.

98. Have your child fingerprinted in case of an emergency.

99. Build a snowperson for every member of your family after the next big snowfall.

100. Try not to work on the weekends so that you can spend time with your child.

101. Have a friendly fight of a different kind with your child—a food fight.

102. Giggle with your child.

103. Plant a tree when your child
     * Is born   * Goes to school
     * Marries   * Becomes a parent

104. Once a month have a day without schedules.
     Just spend time together, relax and unwind
     with your child.

———————♥———————

Every mother is like Moses.
She does not enter the promised land.
She prepares a world she will not see.

Pope Paul VI

———————♥———————

105. Attend a sunrise Easter service with your
     child.

106. Teach your child to take excellent care of
     her teeth.

107. Practice aromatherapy.

108. "Adopt" a foreign child who is in need of assistance through a children's relief organization.

109. Play on a playground together.

110. Buy a story Bible for small children and a lovely leather-bound Bible for older children.

111. Be a good sounding board for your child.

112. Create a home environment that is
     * Fun   * Cheerful
     * Upbeat   * Creative

113. Take a parenting class.

114. Take pride in your child. Show pride in your child.

115. Get good, sound parenting advice from other parents.

116. Give more than you receive.

117. Teach your child that there are angels watching over her.

THE MOST POPULAR TOYS IN THE WORLD

* Dolls
* Puzzles
* Board games
* Trains
* Teddy bears
* Computer games

---

118. Be grateful for your children.

119. Always say, "Bless you," when your child sneezes.

120. Ignore the telephone during family meals and let the answering machine handle the calls.

121. If you pack your child's lunch for school, try to do it the night before so that you won't be as rushed in the morning. It will help to keep you from getting cranky with your family.

122. Teach patriotism.

123. Have a family emergency file in case of a disaster that includes
    * Money
    * Insurance cards
    * Power of attorney for your children
    * Family telephone numbers
    * Family addresses
    * Attorney's name, number, and address

124. Expand your child's world through travel.

125. Let your child learn from his mistakes.

126. Coach your child's teams.

127. Praise more.
    Criticize less.

128. Spend your vacation time with your family.

129. Join the PTA.

130. Sign your letters with X's and O's.

131. Buy classic books for your child.

132. Always say
    * Good morning
    * Good night
    * Good-bye
    To all family members, including four-legged ones.

133. Focus on leaving wonderful memories for your child as your legacy as well as your good name.

134. Lighten up!

135. Send postcards when you are away on business trips.

136. Have a fun fight in the fall leaves.

137. Put up a family bulletin board in your kitchen to help keep the family up to date on
    * Appointments   * Family meetings
    * Engagements   * Good news

138. Teach your child to listen to his intuition.

139. Rent a convertible for your next family outing.

140. Join MADD.

PARENTING QUESTIONS TO ASK YOURSELF

* Do I choose work over family?
* Do I choose friends over family?

141. Stop buying into the quality instead of quantity time myth.

142. Be a mentor to your child's friends.

143. Re-create your happiest times with your child.

144. Compliment your child in front of his friends.

145. Share a hymnal in church with your child.

146. Give two sincere compliments instead of just one to your child.

147. Have a flattering caricature drawn of your child.

148. Learn to forgive and forget. It will make you a better person and a better parent.

149. Be sure that the chores you delegate to your child are age-appropriate.

150. Talk to your child while she is still in the womb.

151. Hold hands with your child during
    * Church   * Long walks
    * Stressful moments * Important talks

152. Teach self-reliance.

153. Keep a first-aid kit in your home and in your car.

154. Hide a kind note in the cookie jar. Your child will surely find it there!

155. Reminisce about fun family times with your child.

156. Nurture your child.

157. Give 200 percent to your child.

158. Ask for hugs from your child.

159. Change your child's room as he grows up.

160. Take the time needed to truly understand your child.

SEEK PROFESSIONAL HELP IF YOUR CHILD IS

* Physically abusive   * Drinks alcohol
* Takes drugs   * Skips school
* Verbally abusive   * Talks about suicide
* Depressed for more than two weeks

161. Be consistent in your
     * Rules   * Behavior
     * Expectations   * Routines

162. Never, ever laugh at your child's dreams.

163. Teach your child to *always* seek God's
     guidance.

164. Learn to bring out the best in your child.

165. Keep a list of all of your child's friends'
     * Names
     * Telephone numbers
     * Addresses

166. Tell the truth and teach your child to do the
     same.

167. Have a family suggestion box.

168. Never allow your child to get a tattoo.

169. Throw an unbirthday party for each family
     member.

170. Give your child self-defense lessons.

What a difference it makes
to come home to a child.

Margaret Fuller

---

171. Blow kisses to your child.

172. Keep the receipts from electronic toys, just
in case of defeats.

173. Trust your child.

174. Teach your child to recycle
    * Toys   * Clothes   * Books
    Have your child give them away to others.

175. Let your child win the game when you play
together while he is young.

176. Keep your parenting style simple.

177. Stay away from negative parents. They will bring your family down.

178. Teach your child to respect all living things.

179. Stop nagging.

GREAT FAMILY DOGS

* Bearded collie
* Bernese mountain dog
* Flat-coated retriever
* Golden retriever
* Labrador retriever
* Newfoundland
* Mutt—save a life by adopting a dog at an animal shelter.

Dogs can add so much love to your child's world!

---

180. Show great enthusiasm for all of your child's accomplishments.

181. Ask for your child's forgiveness when you mess up.

182. Take your child out for an ice cream treat.

183. Always be available when your child needs you.

184. Kiss your child's boo-boos to make them all better.

185. Rub your child's shoulders when she is stressed.

186. Never interrupt your child when he is sharing a story with you.

187. Be your child's hero.

188. Give your baby-sitter
    * Appreciation   * Good pay
    * Bonus or small gift

189. If you suspect that you aren't a good parent, get professional help.

190. Dare to be different from other parents.

191. Celebrate Children's Day in June.

192. Ask the tooth fairy to visit your child when she loses a tooth.

193. Hide gifts within gifts to make them more fun to receive.

194. Have a family game night.

195. Attend concerts in the park with your family.

196. Find out what your child wants for Christmas and tell Santa.

197. Take your child on a tour of your
    * Old neighborhood   * School
    * Childhood church   * Childhood home

198. Never compare your child to others.

199. Develop a family sense of "we-ness."

200. Count your child as one of your most precious blessings.

201. Live by the Ten Commandments and teach your child to do the same.

202. Take a family cruise on the Disney cruise ship, Disney Magic.

203. Be affectionate with your child.

204. Have lots of family cookouts in the summer.

205. Focus on the bright side of parenting.

206. Teach your child to stand up for herself.

PARENTING QUESTIONS TO ASK YOURSELF

* Do I have a role model for the ideal parent? Who is it?
* Who runs our household? Is it the parents or the children?

---

207. Have a scavenger hunt for your child to find a special gift.

208. Serve hot lunches on cold days.

209. Have your child wear a hat in cold weather.

210. Childproof your home.

211. Teenproof your home, too.

212. Teach your child how to deal with
    * Strangers at the door
    * Strangers on the phone

213. Consider getting housekeeping help so that you can spend more time with your child.

214. Serve a balanced diet.

215. Help an overweight child by
    * Cooking light
    * Limiting high-calorie foods
    * Exercising together
    * Serving smaller portions

* Having your child eat slowly
* Not using food as a reward

216. Buy easy care kid's clothes so you won't worry over spots.

217. Don't expect perfection from your child.

———————♥———————

Teach a child to choose the
right path, and when he is grown
he will remain upon it.

Proverbs 22:6

———————♥———————

218. Attend worship service as a family.

219. Sit on a porch swing and get acquainted all over again.

220. Turn a bath into a fun treat with
    * Bubble bath   * Chalk soaps
    * Yellow duckies * Toys
    * Music   * Lush towels

221. Wake up your child using your "happy" voice.

222. Plan a full-moon camp-out in the backyard with the whole family.

223. Bake cookies from scratch together.

224. Turn Sunday suppers into a don't-wanna-miss meal.

225. Sing church hymns at home with your child.

226. Love your mate.

227. Be open with your child.

228. Make fabulous Easter baskets that include
    * Pretty, colorful baskets
    * Grass
    * Chocolate bunnies
    * Bible or other religious book
    * Jelly beans
    * Stuffed bunny

229. Chaperone school events.

230. Listen to your child with your heart.

231. Fly a kite together on a beautiful spring day.

232. Meet with all of your child's teachers.

233. Host a power lunch for you and your child at McDonald's.

234. Teach your child to swim. It might save her life someday.

235. Impress your child by showing her your
     * Trophies   * Awards
     * Honors

236. Write to the White House and request that a birthday card be sent to your child from the President.

237. Teach your child to be color blind about race.

Love is all we have, the only way
that each can help the other.

Euripides

---

238. Surprise your child with a spur-of-the-
moment trip.

239. Move closer to your child's grandparents if
this will bring her more stability in her life.

240. Go Christmas caroling as a family.

241. Teach your child the value of saving.

242. Encourage your child to do his or her part
to save the planet.

243. Help your child to keep a journal.

244. Take your child to the circus.

245. Teach your child to learn the fine art of enjoying solitude.

246. Stop gossiping. Your child may be listening.

247. Plant a garden with your child.

248. Host a kid's block party.

249. Feed the birds together at a nearby park.

250. Mark your calendar with your child's special engagements in red ink.

PARENTING QUESTIONS TO ASK YOURSELF

* What would a child psychologist say about my parenting skills?
* Do I take my parental duties seriously enough?

251. Invest in an Education IRA or an investment fund geared for young investors.

252. Sleep in a barn with your child surrounded by animals.

253. Help to make your child hang-up free by making yourself hang-up free.

254. Have a family talent show.

255. Spend the day together at the zoo.

256. Wish upon a falling star with your child.

257. Read to your child.

258. Send your child to camp, at least once.

259. Play with your child.

260. Build a sandcastle together.

261. Throw a big family-only party.

262. Encourage your child to make friends.

263. Teach your child the meaning of the word "no."

264. Understand that kids have bad days, too.

265. Show your child that you appreciate her efforts in keeping your home neat.

266. Be polite to your child's friends when they call.

267. Don't allow your child to put you, your mate, himself, grandparents, or siblings down.

268. Strive to be a peaceful, calm, loving parent.

269. Allow your child to see you as a human being, not just a parent.

270. Play hooky from work just to spend time with your child.

271. Take your child to a great show at a planetarium.

272. Give your child a five-pound bag of M&M's.

273. Teach your child to spread her wings and fly.

274. Build a gingerbread house with your child.

275. Become a scout leader if your child is into scouting.

276. Design your child's Halloween costume.

277. Take your child to the library regularly.

278. Take tons of home movies.

279. During a nighttime snowfall, sneak out and build a huge snowman for your child to spy in the morning when he gets up.

280. Teach your child to love his community.

———————— ♥ ————————

A baby is an inestimable blessing and better.

Mark Twain

———————— ♥ ————————

281. Help your child compose a letter to Santa.

282. Save for your child's education.

283. Teach your child to save for college.

284. Tell your child all about your day at work.

285. Help your child to express his emotions in a healthy manner.

286. Write new lyrics to your child's favorite song.

287. Give your child educational toys and books.

288. Have family spelling bees.

289. Host family math contests.

290. Support your child's good teachers.

291. Never say things you don't mean.

292. Show your child that he is more important to you than your career or your bank account.

293. Start your child's spiritual education at a tender age.

294. Never treat your child as a possession.

295. Make sure that your child stays in school.

296. Turn Midwinter's Day (February 6) into a big family celebration.

297. Learn the basics of first aid.

298. Celebrate half-birthdays.

299. Serve dessert nightly—yea rah!

300. Stand on your head to talk to your child about a topic that is difficult to bring up. This will break the ice!

———————— ♥ ————————

The most important phase of
living with a person is respect for
that person as an individual.

Millicent Carey McIntosh

———————— ♥ ————————

301. Hold hands with your child on roller coaster
     rides and Ferris wheel rides.

302. Bake a huge birthday cake for your child.

303. Never leave candles burning unattended.

304. Keep in mind that parenting is one of the
     most important jobs in the world.

305. Sing lullabies to your child.

306. Give your child a well-deserved raise in his
     allowance.

307. Put on a puppet show for your child.

308. On a car trip, listen to great children's books on tape.

309. Bring a smile to your child's lips.

310. Stencil your child's bedroom.

311. Watch Saturday morning cartoons together.

312. Just hang out together.

313. Shoot marbles together.

314. Take a class with your child.

315. Understand that all kids get dirty.

316. Teach your child good work ethics.

317. Have a smoke alarm on every floor in your home.

318. Have at least one fire extinguisher in your home and have a monthly family fire drill.

HOW TO MAINTAIN THE SPARK WITH YOUR MATE EVEN THOUGH YOU ARE PARENTS

* Find a good baby-sitter and put her to work at least twice a month for date night
* Have lunch dates while your child is in school
* Put a lock on your bedroom door
* Meet after your child goes to bed
* Get together before your child gets up in the morning
* Hold hands during family times
* Hug a ton
* Call each other during the day
* Send loving notes to each other

Remember—happy parents make for happy kids!

319. Organize all of your family photos into an album to treasure for generations to come.

320. Practice what you preach.

321. Plan a siblings outing for your children at least several times a year.

322. Only allow your child to carpool with safe, responsible drivers.

323. Neatly mend your child's clothes.

324. Keep your friends. You need a life, too. That way you can be a better parent.

325. Play Mozart for young children to improve their brain power.

326. Recharge your child's emotional battery.

327. Have some old-fashioned fun with your child, like
    * Jump rope   * Play hide and seek
    * Play jacks

328. Help your child to be open to new experiences.

329. Take your child to the doctor when she is sick.

330. Teach your child how to pray.

331. Encourage your older child to give her old clothes, books, and toys to her younger siblings.

332. Refrain from being a judgmental and rigid parent.

333. Help school-age children get a good night's sleep, by
    * Not serving caffeine after 3 P.M.
    * Keeping the bedroom less than seventy-five degrees
    * Having a good mattress
    * Not letting your child get too excited before bedtime

334. Set a reasonable curfew for your child.

335. Build a treehouse for your child.

336. Start a compost box in your backyard to teach your child about conservation.

337. Try to keep your distance when your child is having a bad day and wants to be left alone.

338. Do nice things with your child for your mate.

339. Encourage your child to have at least one friend who is elderly.

340. Watch closely what you promise to your children. They are!

341. Ask your child to read a bedtime story to you.

342. Be a cosmopolitan parent and take your child to places like
     * London   * Paris   * New York

343. Have "miracle" parties for your whole family whenever one takes place in your family.

344. Subscribe to the Disney Channel.

345. Hide a loving note in your child's backpack.

346. Insist that your child has excellent school attendance.

PARENTING QUESTIONS TO ASK YOURSELF

* What causes the most friction between me and my child?
* What can I do about it?
* Do I treat my child with the same respect that I show to my friends, coworkers, and other relatives?

347. Give rides to your child's friends when they need them.

348. Create and send a family newsletter to distant relatives with your child's help.

349. Teach your child to be comfortable with who she is.

350. Work to stop child pornography.

351. Explain the dangers of smoking to your child at a young age.

352. Teach your child to pray your favorite prayer.

353. Have Sunday dinners for the entire family.

354. Take a family trip over a long fall weekend instead of waiting till summer.

355. Ask your child for
    * Favors   * Help   * Assistance
    It will make your child feel needed and important.

356. Never go to bed while angry at your child.

357. Never let your child go to bed angry with you.

358. Keep emergency numbers right by the telephone.

359. Learn the Heimlich maneuver to prevent a child from choking.

360. If you must keep guns in your home, be sure that they are locked safely away and are kept unloaded.

361. Plan great parties for your child.

362. Have monogrammed bath towels for each child.

363. Teach your child to keep his promises.

364. Try to make your child's wishes come true.

365. Write a family mission statement and keep it posted in a prominent spot.

366. Dedicate a special space in your home for family prayer, meditation, and reading of Scripture. Place candles and flowers there.

367. Give your child the best education that you can afford.

368. Take your child on a tour of your workplace.

369. Place your child's needs ahead of your own.

370. Never stereotype people in front of your child.

371. Don't compare your child to his friends.

372. Empower your child through fair and wise rules of conduct.

373. Have regular family meetings.

374. Find a mentor for your child.

375. Read what God has to say about parenting in the Bible.

376. Keep in mind that childhood is very short and it happens only once in a lifetime. Make it magical for your child.

377. Never allow your child to hit you or to call you names.

378. Always give candy to your child on
     * Valentine's Day   * Easter
     * Halloween   * Christmas

379. Put signs on the front door to wish your
     child a happy birthday.

380. Take a hike with your child. You might be
     surprised at what conversation pops up
     during your time together.

GREAT PARENTS

* Inspire their children
* Support their children

---

381. Look at what your child is telling you
     through her body language, such as
     * Facial expressions   * Posture
     * Movements   * Hand gestures
     * Way he wears his clothes

382. Watch and learn from other healthy, happy families.

383. Be a very visible person in your child's world.

384. Read holiday stories as a family.

385. Go on your child's field days as a teacher's helper.

386. Have a night light in each
    * Child's room   * Bathroom
    * Hallway   * Stairway

387. Send your child to a camp that focuses solely on your child's hobbies.

388. Have sit-down breakfasts with the whole family.

389. Teach your child to eat fruits and veggies. Try to teach your child to like them!

390. Relax. Parenting isn't brain surgery!

391. Give your child a quality
     * Dictionary   * Thesaurus   * Encyclopedia

392. Start great family traditions.

393. Maintain time-tested family traditions.

394. Read inspiring stories to your children.

395. Never allow your child to dress in an
     inappropriate manner.

396. Drive carefully in school zones.

397. Frame your baby picture along with your
     child's.

398. Color code all family members' things that
     could get mixed up, like
     * Toothbrushes   * Combs
     * Brushes   * Towels
     * Drinking glasses * Notebooks
     * Blankets   * Tote bags

399. Recite poetry to your child.

400. Look at your child through rose-colored glasses when your patience is wearing thin.

401. Hug your child several times a day.

402. Kiss your child good night.

403. Say grace before meals.

404. Plant a living tree in late December to ease the post-holiday blues.

———————— ♥ ————————

Love is swift, sincere, pious,
pleasant, generous, strong, patient,
faithful, prudent, long-suffering,
manly, and never seeking her own;
for wheresoever a man seeketh
his own, there he falleth from love.

Thomas à Kempis

———————— ♥ ————————

405. Dance in the rain with your child on a hot summer day.

406. Make up a positive and inspiring song about your child's life to sing to him when he is feeling sad.

407. Make household chores as enjoyable as possible by
    * Playing music
    * Singing
    * Doing them together
    * Nibbling on a healthy snack
    * Planning them for a convenient time

408. Always treat your child with respect.

409. Teach your child the great dignity of the human soul.

410. Give your child a loving chair—your lap!

411. Write your child's name in icing on the cookies you make.

412. Make your own wonderful-smelling soap to help make bathtime more enjoyable.

413. After a big rain, play in the mud together and make all kinds of messy creations including mud pies.

414. Start saving for your child's future from the day she is born.

415. Teach your child self-love by your own shining example.

416. Save all of the ticket stubs from events that you have attended with your child and give them to her on her sixteenth birthday.

417. Hire a tutor for your child if she is having trouble in school.

418. Help your child to think globally by teaching him about foreign
    * Countries   * Customs
    * Languages

419. Make s'mores together.

420. Cook dinner tonight in the fireplace or outdoors and pretend that you are out camping or are pioneers from the old days.

421. Bake homemade bread in fun, festive shapes.

422. Make sure that young children know
    * Their name
    * Your name
    * Emergency numbers
    * Their address
    * Their telephone number
    * Their state of residence

423. Invent a special holiday for each of your children.

424. If your child is adopted, be sure to celebrate Adoption Day or Family Anniversary Day.

425. Give your child a taste of the good life by
     taking her to
     * The ballet   * The symphony
     * A five-star restaurant * An art museum
     * A fine art gallery   * An elegant boutique

426. The next time that you want to make a
     general criticism of your child, hug him
     instead.

427. Teach your child how to use the Internet
     responsibly.

428. Give your child a book of good jokes, puns,
     and riddles.

429. Work a crossword puzzle together on a lazy
     winter afternoon.

430. Hire a DJ or band for your child's party.

431. Teach your child to think big.

432. Encourage your child to learn lifetime sports, like
    * Golf   * Tennis   * Archery
    * Croquet * Darts

433. Take your child to a county fair.

434. Teach your child about philosophy and psychology.

435. Read the wonderful adventures of Winnie-the-Pooh together.

436. Have a family watermelon-seed-spitting contest.

437. Make sure that your child's vision is tested regularly.

438. Teach your child not to be superstitious.

439. Take your child to the Olympics to inspire her to feats of greatness.

440. Hunt for buried treasure together.

PARENTING QUESTIONS TO ASK YOURSELF

* If I died today, what regrets would I have regarding my child?
* What would my legacy mean to my child?
* Do I have in place a plan to take care of my child if something happens to me?
* Do I have a will?

441. Have your child wear protective gear when
    * Rollerblading   * Bicycling
    * Mountain climbing   * Playing hockey

442. Understand the dangers for young children playing contact sports.

443. When the family gets a pet, let your child name it.

444. Encourage your child's interest in technology by giving him an interactive computer toy.

445. Totally accept your child, faults and all!

446. Teach your child to speak a foreign language and open up a whole new world for him.

447. Make a donation to the Toys for Tots Campaign in honor of your child. Call your nearest Marine base for details.

448. Write down your child's locker combination for it might come in handy someday.

449. Wake your child up with a kiss.

450. Have a Nonsensical Day and let your child run wild.

451. Always look over your child's report cards.

452. Encourage your parents to set up a trust fund for their grandchild.

453. Get rid of all of the clutter around your house.

454. Keep your personal papers in order.

455. Carry life insurance on your child to prevent financial problems for your family.

456. Be sure to carry life insurance on you and your spouse.

457. Start a collection of antique children's books for your child. It may be quite valuable when he is grown.

458. Rearrange your accessories and furniture for a nice family pick-me-up.

459. Show your children how people of all social status live.

460. Take your child to the orthodontist if you feel that he could benefit from wearing braces.

461. Give yourself a nice Mother's Day or Father's Day gift. Okay, I snuck this one in just for the sake of the parents. After all, you must be a great parent if you are reading about loving your child!

462. Help your child to make New Year's resolutions.

463. Have a good reading lamp on your child's desk.

464. Try with all of your heart to give your child two loving parents.

465. Host a family talent show and be sure to include grandparents, cousins, aunts, and uncles.

466. Teach your child to be respectful of the neighbors.

467. Look for your child's hidden talents.

468. Teach your child to go after the brass ring.

469. Never overschedule your child's time. It makes life way too stressful for children and parents.

470. Take your child to a mystery dinner at a local playhouse and let your child solve the whodunit.

———————— ♥ ————————

We have two ears and one mouth
so that we can listen as much
as we speak.

Epictetus

———————— ♥ ————————

471. Make sure that your child *always* wears his seat belt and set a good example by always wearing yours.

472. Watch your child while she is sleeping and you will feel so much love for her.

473. Never say never or you may live to regret it.

474. Make homemade holiday decorations together.

475. Keep a good, current photograph of your child along with her height and weight in a safe place in case of an emergency.

476. If your family dog gets lost, keep looking for it until it is found. Don't give up or you will break your child's heart.

477. Teach your child what to do if he becomes lost.

478. Do some research on your local hospitals to determine which have pediatric-size equipment available in an emergency.

479. Try not to talk too much about the office during family meals.

480. Never expose your child to secondhand smoke.

481. Keep these little rewards for good behavior on hand so that you can use them at appropriate moments:
    * Puzzles
    * Small games
    * McDonald's gift certificates
    * Books
    * Magazines
    * Bookmarks
    * Interesting pens and pencils

482. Allow your child to stay up past his bedtime on special occasions.

483. Never give only underwear for a birthday or Christmas gift.

484. Teach your child to take the road less traveled.

485. Play comedy tapes in the car on the way to school to get your child in a good mood.

486. Teach your child to be reliable. Show them that you are.

487. Help your child not to develop the worry habit.

488. Do some aerobic type exercise as a family.

489. Write down all of your goals for your child. Ask yourself if you are being realistic. Ask yourself if you are being self-serving. Be honest with yourself.

490. Encourage your child to invite her friends to attend worship services with your family.

491. Get married all over again in the presence of your children.

492. Treat your family like a well-run corporation and use these management strategies:
    * Coaching   * Leading
    * Teaching   * Inspiring

493. Make sure that your child receives the proper immunizations against childhood diseases.

494. Refrain from the following activities while pregnant:
    * Smoking
    * Drinking alcohol
    * Taking drugs
    * Using medications without your doctor's approval
    * Drinking beverages with caffeine in them

495. Deal appropriately with your child's bully.

496. Take your child to Washington, D.C.

497. Listen to your child practice his speech and be fascinated by it.

498. Teach your child how to apologize.

499. Take your child to visit a pet store. Let him buy a gift for that special member of the family.

500. Savor every moment that you get to spend with your child.

501. Place a loving note inside a helium-filled balloon.

502. When your child gives you a present:
    * Use it or wear it right away
    * Gush over it
    * Send a thank-you note to your child
    * Treasure it

503. Applaud your child's talents.

504. Never be jealous of the attention your spouse shows to your child.

505. Help your child to write
    * Letters   * Poems
    * Songs   * In a journal

506. Tell your child what you have learned from your mistakes.

507. Rent a tandem for the next pretty afternoon.

———————— ♥ ————————

Trust yourself. You know more
than you think you do.

Dr. Benjamin Spock

———————— ♥ ————————

508. Teach your child to respect members of the
opposite sex.

509. Understand that in parenting actions do
speak louder than words.

510. Give several rounds of praise for every
piece of criticism that you dish out.

511. Have family standards, like
   * Unconditional love   * Respect
   * Sense of family community * Loyalty
   * Truthfulness

512. Ask your child to read to you.

513. Help your child plan a party for his friends.

514. Teach your children how to behave in public by your good example.

515. On cold days have your child dress in layers.

516. Start a family gratitude journal where all family members write what they are most grateful for within your family. Keep it out and make it an ongoing family project. Everyone will benefit from reading and writing in it.

517. Never compete with the other parent for your child's love. Make that a mind game that you just won't play.

518. To avoid trouble on city streets, teach your child to walk quickly and with a sense of purpose.

519. Understand that your child is
   * Unique
   * Special
   * An individual with his own perspective
   * God's creation

520. Always accompany your child to the doctor.

PARENTING QUESTIONS TO ASK YOURSELF

* Do I attend my child's after-school activities? If not, how can I change that?
* Is there any way that I could stay at home with my child and be a full-time parent?
* Could I get more involved in my child's life?

521. Turn your living room into a big campground by using sheets for a tent and get out your old sleeping bags. Have the entire family "camp" all night together. Sing songs, tell stories, and munch on junk food.

522. Have a sunrise doughnut breakfast on the back porch together.

523. Keep in mind that your child is a child and not a miniature adult.

524. Take lots of family getaway weekends.

525. Have a "girls' night out" for all female family members, including
    * Mom   * Daughters
    * Aunts   * Grandmothers
    * Cousins

526. Have a "boys' night out" for all male family members, including
    * Dad   * Sons
    * Uncles   * Grandpas
    * Cousins

527. Shop at a five-and-dime store and let the kids pick out some fun, little toys.

528. Say nice things about your child to his friends.

529. Have a beloved family pet and teach your child to treat it with
    * Love　　　　* Kindness
    * Respect　　　* Dignity

530. Talk to your child about not drinking alcohol.

531. Have your child's portrait painted by a well-known artist.

532. Teach your child to floss her teeth and therefore save her from dental problems down the road.

533. Try to find new activities that you can do with your child.

534. Be old-fashioned and take a Sunday afternoon drive together.

535. Wrap your child's birthday presents in extra-special papers and ribbons.

536. Make zillions of holiday cookies.

537. Teach your child to keep
     * Promises   * Secrets
     * Commitments

538. Help to ease your child's emotional and
     physical growing pains.

539. Buy good-tasting cough drops for your
     child when she has a cough.

540. Take your child to visit the countries of her
     ancestors.

541. Teach your child the wonderful art of
     positive self-talk.

542. Give your child a replica of your favorite
     childhood toy.

543. Read the warning labels on all toys that you
     buy for your child. Many toys are not for
     small children because they could be a
     choking hazard.

544. Encourage your child to do things for himself.

545. Send your child to vacation Bible school.

THE MOST COMMON PARENTING MISTAKES

* Failure to communicate with the child
* Failure to listen to the child's point of view
* Failure to change what isn't working in the family unit
* Failure to give love freely

546. Keep a scrapbook of the changes in your child's room decor through the years.

547. Remember that you don't have to be a perfect parent.

548. Try not to place your child's bed on an outside wall for it is usually the coldest wall in the room.

549. Plant a living Easter basket for your child.

550. Have a change of seasons celebration.

551. When you name your child think it through from every angle. After all, your child will carry that name for all of the days of his life.

552. Play fun, kind-spirited April Fool's Day jokes with your child.

553. Sing "You've Got a Friend" to your child at bedtime.

554. Teach your child to have a high opinion of herself.

555. Act "as if" you are a fabulous parent and you will be.

556. Make the most out of today for your child's sake.

557. Write a loving message in calligraphy and frame it for your child.

558. Teach your child to lose with grace and dignity.

559. Live a good, honorable, fun-filled life.

560. Take your child to visit and worship in
    * Country churches   * Shrines/temples
    * Grand cathedrals   * Synagogues

561. Remember the three C's of parenting—courage and commitment from the cradle.

562. Take your child to a place that he has never been to before.

563. Organize important family documents, like
    * Wills   * Insurance forms
    * Birth certificates   * Marriage license
    * Tax returns   * Warranties
    * Family genealogy

564. Get your child's clothes for school laid out and ready the night before.

565. Turn off the television during
     * Breakfast   * Lunch
     * Dinner   * Family meetings
     * Important talks

566. Set high standards for yourself.
     Set high standards for your children.

567. Stay with your child when she is in the hospital.

A torn jacket is soon mended;
but hard words bruise the
heart of a child.

Henry Wadsworth Longfellow

---

568. Understand the rules of the games you play with your child.

569. Have a picture of your family taken in an instant photo booth.

570. Take your child to a beautiful state park.

571. Listen to your child's
    * Fears   * Troubles
    * Worries   * Concerns
    Use the same amount of respect that you give your friends or spouse when they talk to you.

572. Teach your child to show respect when an older person enters the room by standing up.

573. Send the following types of holiday cards to your child:
    * Valentine's Day   * Easter
    * Halloween   * Thanksgiving
    * Christmas   * Hanukkah

574. Let go and let God handle your parenting worries.

575. Take your dog to obedience school so that he will be a better pet for your child.

576. Understand that your child is not an exact copy of you.

577. If you don't know the answer to your child's question, find someone who does.

There is always one moment
in childhood when the door opens
and lets the future in.

Graham Greene

---

578. Make parenting a little bit easier by carrying
    * Breath mints   * Band-Aids
    * Hand sanitizers   * Handi Wipes

579. If your child mows the grass, have him wear steel-toed shoes.

580. Help your child with his homework. This might mean just encouraging your child to get it done.

581. Champion children's causes in your
    * Family   * City
    * Neighborhood   * Country
    * World

582. Say what you mean.
    Mean what you say.

583. Buy a cute step stool so that your child can easily reach things.

584. Send a singing telegram to your child.

585. Stop all family arguments that get out of hand. Talk later after everyone has calmed down.

586. Photograph your child all over town. You will treasure these photos forever.

587. Put down this book and go and hug your child.

588. Write a poem of love to your child.

589. Plan to leave work early tomorrow to spend more time with your child.

590. Engrave all pieces of jewelry that you give to your child. Later these items will become sentimental treasures.

591. Buy matching T-shirts for you and your child.

592. Wish on a new moon with your child every month.

593. Share all gifts of food that you receive with your child.

594. Buy gifts that hold a special meaning for your child.

595. Make it a three-day weekend and spend it with your family.

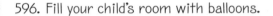

Men are what their mothers made them.

Ralph Waldo Emerson

596. Fill your child's room with balloons.

597. Ask the Easter Bunny to visit your house at Easter.

598. Explain to your child all about your religious beliefs.

599. Host a wintertime picnic in the snow and serve hot cocoa and yummy warm treats.

600. Dye Easter eggs and write each child's name on them.

601. Help your child to set lifelong goals to make this world a better place.

602. Take your child to a professional sporting event.

603. After your child's big game host a great tailgate party for friends, family, team members, and their parents.

604. Write a love letter to your child and send it through the mail.

605. Help your child to accept any weaknesses that can't be overcome.

606. Explore a cave together and have a big adventure.

607. Have a special afternoon tea in a grand old hotel together.

608. Meander through a craft fair arm in arm and buy a homemade gift for your child.

609. Take a family vacation aboard a train. You'll have lots of time for good conversation.

610. Never let your child see you being petty or vindictive.

611. Host a junk food family party once a month and encourage all family members to bring their yummy favorites.

612. Pick up litter and recycle to set a good example for your child.

613. Sing camp songs in the backyard late in the evening as a family.

614. Rent the best family movies for a film festival.

615. Invite a foreign exchange student to come and live with you and show the world in a personal manner to your child.

616. Take your child shopping at an FAO Schwarz store.

617. If you can, arrange for your child to meet his hero.

618. Start a quilt when your child is born and give it to her on her fifth birthday when she is old enough to really appreciate it.

619. Start a reading group for kids in your neighborhood.

620. Take your child to ride bumper cars.

621. Take your child on a jeep ride through the desert. Your child will love the change of scenery.

It is easier to build a child
than to repair an adult.

Author Unknown

---

622. Play your old childhood favorites, like
    * Monopoly   * Clue
    * Sorry   * Masterpiece
    * Twister   * Chutes and Ladders

623. Take your child to Colonial Williamsburg and let her experience our nation's history firsthand.

624. Hide a box of candy under your child's pillow.

625. Display great schoolwork and artwork on the family refrigerator.

626. Check to be sure that the other parent is very involved in your child's life.

627. Invite your child's friends over on a regular basis.

628. Make your home a fun place for kids to be.

629. Teach your child that failure is just part of the learning process and not a major catastrophe.

630. Avoid trying to live your life through your child's accomplishments.

631. Send your child a get well card when she is sick.

632. When dealing with your child, don't
    * Scream
    * Hit
    * Name call

633. Encourage your child to play outside in the fresh air.

634. Cultivate a love of books in your child.

635. Do your child a favor by not resorting to bad examples of your behavior from your childhood to prove a point. After all, the world has changed a great deal since then.

636. Keep your word to every member of your family, including your parents.

637. Be very careful about whom you ask to look after your child.

638. Talk to your child at his level of
     understanding.

639. Key parenting phrases:
     * "I love you"
     * "I'm glad you are my child"
     * "Thanks"
     * "Please"
     * "Good job"

PARENTING QUESTIONS TO ASK YOURSELF

When was the last time that you made
your child
     * Laugh?
     * Happy?
     * Cry?

When was the last time you gave your
child a
     * Hug?
     * Kiss?
     * Kind word?

---

640. Spend the day together at the beach.

641. Treat your child to a midweek
    * Movie   * Dinner out on the town
    * Mini shopping spree

642. Instead of nagging, leave little cute notes to remind your child to do his chores.

643. Understand that when your child is ill, stressed, or tired, she is much more likely to be grumpy. Try to take it in stride.

644. Learn to say, "I love you," in different languages.

645. Apologize when you mess up in your parenting responsibilities.

646. Take pride in your home and your yard.

647. Start the day with a prayer that you say with your child.

648. Have a pillow fight with your child.

649. Get on the floor and playfully wrestle with your child.

650. Talk about spiritual matters during family meals.

651. Get rid of emotional trash in your home, like:
     * Trashy novels   * R-rated movies
     * Inappropriate CDs   * Lewd magazines

652. Break out of your dinnertime conversation rut. Talk about new, exciting topics.

653. Turn down unnecessary business and social invitations so that you can spend more time with your family.

654. Save buttons from your child's clothes and use them to decorate a frame for a special photo of him.

655. Make a donation in your child's name to her favorite charity.

656. Host an elegant dinner party for your child's friends.

657. Take your child to visit his neighbors:
* Canada
* Mexico

658. Teach your child that just one person can make a huge difference in our world.

659. Give your child a ten-pound bag of popcorn in her favorite flavor.

660. Serve breakfast by candlelight on a dark winter's morning.

661. Write out your favorite family recipes for your child.

662. Spend a Saturday afternoon together sailing remote-controlled boats on a nearby lake.

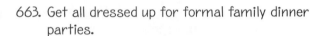

A good example is the best sermon.

Anonymous

663. Get all dressed up for formal family dinner parties.

664. Teach your child that crime doesn't pay by taking him on a tour of your local jail.

665. Teach your child not to pick up hitchhikers.

666. Be a sponsor for your child's team.

667. Turn off the lights and watch a summer thunderstorm together.

668. During tornado warnings make sure that your family takes shelter.

669. This Saturday night, paint the town red with your family.

670. Before a child attends a funeral, prepare your child emotionally.

671. Make a clover necklace for your child while the two of you play outside.

672. If you live in the city, spend the weekend at a quaint bed and breakfast in the country.

673. Set firm and fair rules for your child about how he should behave with his friends in your home.

Even a bad match can beget good children.

Jewish Saying

---

674. Take your child to the great Smithsonian.

675. Encourage your child to try out for different teams and clubs.

676. Make homemade dessert pizza together and let your child use her creativity to decorate it.

677. Help your child to meet all school deadlines.

678. Write notes of praise and encouragement to your child's teacher.

679. Send your child a cookie bouquet.

680. Buy your child a gift just because you love him.

681. Create matching party costumes for the entire family.

682. Teach your child not to tease other children.

683. Help your child to conquer her fears.

684. Hang a "Home Sweet Home" sign in your house.

685. Serve fresh fruits and vegetables that are in season and grown locally.

686. Watch these classic movies with your family:
    * Mary Poppins
    * The Wizard of Oz
    * The Sound of Music
    * It's a Wonderful Life

687. Even if your children must share a room, try to create a space for each child that he can call his own.

688. Take your child to see the Christmas tree at the White House.

689. Don't cheat when you play games with your child.

690. Name your cabin in honor of your child.

691. Buy your child theme sweatshirts for
    * Valentine's Day   * Halloween
    * Christmas

692. Create an eye-catching centerpiece for your table.

693. Take your child to see a 3-D movie at an IMAX theater.

694. Make a meal out of just desserts.

695. Encourage your child to find her true calling in life.

696. Communicate with distant relatives over the Internet with your child.

697. Go ice skating with your child at Christmastime.

698. Talk to your child about sex.

699. Leave a nice message on your answering machine for your child to hear when he gets home.

💜

Children without a childhood
are tragic.

Mendele Mocher Seforim

💜
---

700. Go skateboarding with your child.

701. Consider the big risks regarding your child's safety before you allow her to jump on a trampoline.

702. Teach your child how our local, state, and national governments operate.

703. Dedicate a song on the radio to your child.

704. Watch a mother bird feed her babies together.

705. Talk your parents into giving their old toys to your child.

706. Burn candles at the dinner table tonight to set a special mood.

707. Encourage your child to forgive any mistakes he makes. Self-forgiveness is one of the keys to happiness.

PARENTING QUESTIONS TO ASK YOURSELF

When was the last time that you told your child that you
* Loved him?
* Were proud of him?
* Were glad that he is your child?

Would I want to have myself as my own parent?

When was the last time that I went out alone with my child and did something fun?

---

708. Hook a colorful rug for your child's bedroom.

709. Tell your child about all of your accomplishments as a young person.

710. Be patient with your child's friends.

711. Try your very best to keep your child safe.

712. Make a list of all of the things that you wish that you had known as a child and give it to your child.

713. Teach your child to be independent.

714. Sew a homemade toy for your child.

715. Spend weekends meandering the back roads of our country together.

716. Encourage your child's grandparents to give praise lavishly, but honestly to your child.

717. Live each day in love.

718. Celebrate Common Sense Day (January 29) by talking about the value of using your head to rule your actions.

719. Bronze your child's baby shoes.

HOW WELL DO YOU KNOW YOUR CHILD?

Do You Know Your Child's Favorite

✻ Color	✻ Book	✻ Toy
✻ Sport	✻ TV show	✻ Pastime
✻ Song	✻ Memory	✻ Teacher
✻ Subject	✻ Friend	✻ Holiday
✻ Movie	✻ Entertainer	✻ Meal
✻ Time of day	✻ Dessert	✻ CD
✻ Season	✻ Store	✻ Activity
✻ Vacation spot		

720. Serve a healthy after-school snack.

721. Let your child give you a respectful nickname if she wants to for special occasions.

722. Say, "I love you." in sign language to your child across a crowded room.

723. Answer letters addressed to
     * Santa   * Easter Bunny
     * Cupid   * Tooth Fairy
     If the above are too busy to handle all of their mail.

724. Help your child to experience the kindness of strangers.

725. Allow your child to call friends who live out of town.

726. Tuck your child into bed at night when she is young.

727. Teach your child the difference between right and wrong.

728. Read between the lines when your child talks to you about a serious topic.

729. Laugh until you cry with your child.

730. Give a huge, all-day sucker to your child.

731. Give a plastic pumpkin filled with yummy candy the week before Halloween to get the holiday attitude rolling.

732. Teach your child to avoid naysayers.

733. Teach your child not to waste
    * Time   * Food
    * Money   * Energy

734. Call your child just to say hello.

735. Frame your child's baby picture along with her baby bracelet.

736. Build colossal cheeseburgers for a family cookout.

737. Pray for your child
    * Morning
    * Noon
    * Night

738. Help your child shop for gifts for Grandparents' Day.

739. Make your child feel important by asking his opinion.

740. Drive carefully, especially when your child is in the car.

741. Never, ever drink and drive.

742. Limit the number of TVs in your home.

743. Introduce your child proudly to your acquaintances.

744. Give a tape to your child of her favorite movie so that she can see it whenever she wants.

745. Remember that all kids want recognition and praise.

746. Buy a cool lunch box for your child before school starts.

747. Send your child a loving fax.

748. Send your child a loving E-mail.

749. Host a cookout for your child and her pals.

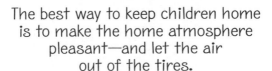

The best way to keep children home
is to make the home atmosphere
pleasant—and let the air
out of the tires.

Dorothy Parker

750. Pick your child up from school for a special
     lunch.

751. Take your child on a shopping spree.

752. Get a great-looking backpack for your child
     to use for carrying his homework home
     from school.

753. Give your child extra support during
    stressful times:
    * First week of school
    * When a close friend moves away
    * Tryouts are being held for teams, etc.
    * You and your spouse are having
        difficulties of any kind
    * The family is moving
    * Death of a relative
    * A family member is seriously ill
    * Your beloved family pet is ill or dies

754. Hide a silver dollar in each of her shoes
    during the night.

755. Host a family "Special Dress Day" once
    every few months. Try
    * Hawaiian Day
    * PJ Day
    * Anything Goes Day
    * Clothes On Backwards Day
    * Seventies Day

756. If your child lives in another city, get a toll-free telephone number so he can call you whenever he wants.

757. Encourage a young artist by doing the following together:
    * Coloring   * Finger-painting
    * Making doodle art

758. Teach your child to be fair and just.

759. Put in the extra effort that is needed to create beautiful memories for your child.

760. Try to live out your childhood dreams as a wonderful example that dreams do come true.

761. Know that real love doesn't spoil a child.

762. Teach your child all of these virtues:
    * Charity   * Faith   * Fairness
    * Self-discipline * Courage   * Respect
    * Love   * Honesty   *Helpfulness
    * Compassion

763. Go for a family walk after dinner.

764. Be kind to the family pet. Your child will learn so much about kindness to animals.

765. Review your child's school records.

766. Understand that parenting means being with your child.

767. Work on improving your energy level so that you will enjoy your role as a parent even more. Try
    * Exercising   * Praying
    * Eating well   * Getting eight hours sleep

768. Help your child to get in touch with his feelings by asking:
    * What do you want?
    * How do you want things to turn out?
    * In your heart of hearts, what feels right?

769. Surprise your child in big and small but always fun ways.

———— ♥ ————

Rule No. 1 is, don't sweat the small stuff.
Rule No. 2 is, it's all small stuff.

Robert Eliot

———— ♥ ————

770. Teach your child that when God is on your side, one is a majority.

771. Never leave your young child unattended in a parked car.

772. Schedule a weekly appointment with each child. Mark it on your calendar.

773. Take your child to visit lots of universities to inspire and inform her.

774. Make a huge difference in the quality of your child's life by improving the state of your relationship with your mate.

775. Make your child write thank-you notes for gifts.

776. Have serious talks outdoors. Natural settings can be so relaxing.

777. Use the power of touch with your child.

778. Help your child pack for trips.

779. Put your child's name and address inside his luggage.

780. Have twin prints made of all special events that involve your child. Let your child send the copies to friends and relatives.

781. Hold your young child's hand when you cross the street.

782. Buy a good mattress for your child's bed.

783. Create a relaxing ritual for your child with a
   * Bubble bath
   * Candlelight bath
   * Sweet oil bath

784. Teach your child to stop and smell the roses.

785. Think of parenthood as your own spiritual mission.

786. Give your child one of your most valuable resources—your time.

787. Have picnics in unusual places, like
    * In your car   * On rooftops
    * In treehouses   * By the pool
    * In museum gardens

788. Write a song for your child.

789. Save all of the cards, letters, and poems that your child gives to you.

790. Turn a wonderful family photo into a neat poster.

791. Have a family night out at least once a month.

792. Make easy, but good Rice Krispies treats in fun holiday shapes and colors.

793. Work hard to earn your child's trust.

794. Work even harder to keep your child's trust.

795. Give tons of TLC.

796. Make the necessary sacrifices and be a stay-at-home parent.

797. Treat your child to a designer garment.

798. Allow your child to cry on your shoulder during sad moments.

799. Try new family activities to make life more fun for all family members.

800. Include the family pet in all the family activities that you possibly can.

HOW TO KEEP UP WITH YOUR FRIENDS AND STILL BE A GREAT PARENT

* Invite your friends to your home
* Meet for breakfast on Saturdays and have your spouse watch the kids
* Call your friends on the telephone often
* Meet for coffee during school hours
* Run errands together
* Take family outings with your family and your friend's family
* Attend church together with both families

Remember—you'll feel more loving toward your child when your social needs are met.

801. Prepare welcome home dinners for your child when he comes home from camp or trips.

802. Have your child invite a friend to spend the night.

803. Plan a get-reacquainted party for your child and her friends the week before school starts.

804. Set up a parents neighborhood support group.

805. If you have a swimming pool, be sure to have a locked fence around it.

806. Never leave your child unattended in a swimming pool.

807. Teach your child good grooming habits.

808. Get your child a stylish, flattering haircut.

809. When you can't be home to watch, tape programs on parenting skills to view when you have the time.

810. Encourage your child to pray for his future mate's well-being.

811. Help your child remember the true meaning of Christmas.

812. Learn nonviolent ways of disciplining your child.

813. Read the true stories of angels on earth in Guidepost's *Angels on Earth* magazine. It will build faith and give comfort to your child.

814. Take a big interest in your child's
    * Hobbies   * Friends
    * After-school activities   * Schoolwork

815. Write your own parent's creed.

816. Write down ten qualities that you want your child to identify in you. Keep the list as an emotional road map and refer to it often.

817. Turn off the alarm and let your child sleep late whenever you can.

818. Write down all of the things that your parents did right in raising you and try to incorporate those into your parenting.

819. To keep your child running on time, give your child
   * An alarm clock
   * A wristwatch

820. Ask your child to describe his dream parents. Listen with open ears and heart. Use the new information to better your parenting skills.

———— ♥ ————

The ordinary arts we practice every day
at home are of more importance
to the soul than their simplicity
might suggest.

Thomas Moore

———— ♥ ————

821. Improve your child's confidence by showing him the joy of personal accomplishments.

822. Don't be naive and expect your child to fully
     take care of your family's pets. Ninety
     percent of all parents end up with those
     responsibilities despite what their children
     have promised.

823. When you can't afford the toy or fashions
     that your child is clamoring for, try
     * Shopping sales
     * Trading items among family members
     * Asking your child to pay for part of it
     * Browsing secondhand shops
     * Shopping yard sales
     * Trading items with friends
     * Borrowing the item

824. Are you feeling overwhelmed? Get help
     from your
     * Spouse   * Siblings
     * Neighbors   * Parents
     * Grandparents   * Minister
     * Mental health professionals

———————♥———————

Children are likely to live up to
what you believe of them.

Lady Bird Johnson

———————♥———————

825. Give your child a cheer-up gift after he has
a really bad day.

826. Name your boat after your child.

827. Give your child a "first" cookbook to inspire
a love of cooking.

828. Be fun.

829. Set up your home computer to protect
your child from pornography.

830. Take a family journey of a lifetime. Take a
ride on a hot air balloon.

831. Teach your child not to give out personal
information over the phone or Internet.

832. Show extra tenderness when your child is sick or hurt.

833. Buy what your child's friends are selling whether it is lemonade or Girl Scout cookies. This way you will be a good guy and encourage other parents to buy from your child.

834. Admit it when you and your spouse have shown bad judgment regarding family matters.

835. Play a game of family hide-and-seek.

836. "Adopt" a resident of a nursing home who is lonely and visit him with your child.

837. Set an important educational example by continuing your education.

838. Teach your child to be true to himself.

839. Give your child a copy of The Wish List by Barbara Ann Kipfer to encourage her to dream big dreams.

840. Teach your child that the majority of mistakes can be rectified and not to make a mountain out of a molehill.

Ah! There's nothing like staying home for real comfort.

Jane Austen

---

841. Participate in all that your community offers for children's learning and entertainment.

842. Write the names of everyone in your photographs as well as the date on the back of each picture. Years from now your child will be glad that you did.

843. Teach your child to reach out to kids in need. Teach him that there are emotional, spiritual, and financial needs in your community.

844. Have your child invite her grandparents to a grandparents/grandchild type of event.

845. Wake your child up with music. It is a great way to start the day.

846. Use colorful stamps when you mail things to your child.

847. Take spring breaks with your family.

848. Teach your child to sing the old, classic songs.

849. Have a comfortable reading chair in your child's room.

850. No matter what your child does, keep your heart open to him.

851. Light a candle in church for your child.

852. Host a formal family Thanksgiving dinner with all the trimmings.

853. Teach your child to build on his successes.

854. Have your child write down ten to twenty goals for himself. Help your child to reach them.

855. Teach your child that the Kingdom of God is within her.

856. Explain to your child that violence is not a solution to problems.

857. Repeat good parenting affirmations throughout your day.

858. Write out your parenting affirmations again and again. This will drive them home.

859. Offer your helping hand to your child when he needs it.

860. When you give a compliment to your child, make it specific.

861. When your child is bored, give activity suggestions that do not include television as an option.

PARENTING QUESTIONS TO ASK YOURSELF

* Do I practice what I preach?
* Are my friends setting a good example for my child?
* Have I ever let my child down? Could I make it up to him?

862. Teach your child to be curious.

863. Set up situations that allow your child to shine.

864. Place happy family snapshots throughout your home.

865. For dads only—make your child a priority before your
    * Career   * Friends
    * Sports   * Hobbies
    * TV viewing time * Community work

866. Never pigeonhole your child's personality. After all, kids are very complex beings.

867. Hang a chalkboard near the back door to leave messages for your child.

868. Send a gigantic greeting card.

869. Give your child an oversized coloring book when your child is sick and needs to stay quiet.

870. Take your child along on your next business trip.

871. Ask Santa to come by your home on Christmas Eve and be sure to leave out milk and cookies for him.

872. On your child's birthday, have a special
meal for
* Breakfast   * Lunch   * Dinner

873. Spend the next sixty minutes doting on
your child.

874. Make gifts extra special by wrapping them
in
* Scarves   * Mufflers   * T-shirts
* Bandannas   * Sweats

875. Instead of sleeping late on Sunday
mornings, attend church with your child.

876. Don't turn it into "us" versus "them" when
it comes to parents and children.

877. Cook favorite foods from your childhood.

878. Make a two-person support team for your
child composed of you and your mate.

879. Never let your child hear you or your mate
threaten each other with divorce.

880. Buy matching PJs for the whole family.

———— ♥ ————

Love gives itself, it is not bought.

Henry Wadsworth Longfellow

———— ♥ ————

881. At Halloween, take your child to a pumpkin farm to get your jack-o'-lantern instead of going to the supermarket.

882. Talk to your kids about drugs before it is too late.

883. If your child is having trouble with his schoolwork, send him to a learning center.

884. Teach your child not to let his friends make his decisions for him.

885. Give your child a standing ovation every time she performs in public.

886. Take your child to visit a horse farm to have his first riding lesson.

887. Never use physical punishments. It teaches your child that violence is the proper response.

888. Consider moving closer to your child's aunts, uncles, and cousins.

889. If your child is in day care, be sure that it is a quality facility.

890. Turn off controversial talk shows when your child is at home.

891. Give your child a subscription to a quality child's magazine.

892. Take your child to the best bakery in town and let him order the treat of his choice.

893. Buy a raffle ticket for something that your child would like to win.

894. Buy clothes that appeal to your child and not just to you.

895. Turn your child's artwork into a needlepoint or cross-stitch pillow by transferring the design onto the canvas.

896. Buy a fun mouse pad for your child's computer.

897. Keep yourself in good physical condition. Hey, your child wants you around for many years to come!

898. Teach your child when to mind his own business.

899. Vote in every election to teach your child the importance of this privilege.

900. Paint a chalk masterpiece with your child on the front walk.

901. Take your child to see a Shakespearean play. Start early to cultivate a love of the classics.

902. Tuck a love note or compliment in your child's lunch bag.

903. Let your child draw your portrait. You will learn a lot about how your child views you.

904. Teach your child not to be a whiner or complainer.

905. Whenever you can, let your child choose what she is going to wear.

If you want your children to improve, let them overhear the nice things you say about them.

Haim Ginott

---

906. Try to imagine how big, old, and powerful you seem to your child.

907. Explain things to your child. Yes, it takes extra effort and time, but your child will benefit immensely from your wisdom.

908. Spend the day at a park and
    * Explore trails   * Play on the swing sets
    * Throw Frisbees   * Have a picnic

909. Take a break from the local and national news programs when young children are in the room and something disturbing has taken place in the world.

910. Go for a leisurely stroll around your neighborhood with your child.

911. Keep a lock on your bedroom door to prevent embarrassing moments.

912. Help everyone in your family get a good night's sleep by
    * Talking quietly and peacefully at bedtime
    * Serving hot cocoa near bedtime
    * Giving all family members a good quality pillow

913. Celebrate and embrace the concept of simplicity in your family's lives.

914. Joke with your child.

915. Look for all of the things that your child has done right in the recent past. Compliment him on these things.

916. Properly prioritize your life:
    * God   * Family   * Career

917. Show respect and understanding for your child's feelings of puppy love.

918. Never talk badly about your mate in front of your child.

919. Show your child good work ethics by your own example.

920. Take your child on a "free" vacation by trading homes with a sibling, parent, or friend.

---❤---

Children have more need of models than of critics.

Joseph Joubet

---❤---

921. Help your child make a holiday wreath for your car's front grill.

922. Run holiday errands for your children.

923. Ask God to show you ways to help your child.

924. Place a small Christmas tree in your child's room.

925. Sew an heirloom Christmas stocking for each child.

926. Watch your child's behavior for signs of drug or alcohol abuse.

927. Have a heart-to-heart talk with your child today.

928. Give your child a hardcover copy of *Charlotte's Web* by E. B. White. It is one of the best children's stories ever written.

929. Buy a darling cookie jar for your kitchen and keep it filled with yummy cookies.

930. Split a banana split with your child for dinner tonight.

931. Tell your child regularly that you thank God for her.

932. Teach your child to keep his room relatively clean at all times. It will make your life and his much easier and more pleasant for both of you.

933. Take the family to the nearest pool and have a family swimming party.

934. Help a lost dog to find a good home and teach your child a life lesson in compassion.

935. Talk to your child about his views on what a fair allowance would be.

936. Keep in mind that God is listening to you when you talk to your child. Ask yourself if that is a comforting thought or a scary one.

937. Teach little ones to be gentle with
    * Babies   * The aged
    * Animals   * Fine things
    * Expensive toys   * Electronics
    * Others' feelings   * Smaller children

938. Give your child a foot massage.

939. Put your child's needs ahead of your own.

940. Take your child to a greenhouse and allow her to purchase a houseplant to care for in her room.

941. Try to say yes every time that you can.

PARENTING QUESTIONS TO ASK YOURSELF

* Can my child always talk freely with me?
* Do I soothe my child's fears? Am I a source of fear?
* Do I lose my temper with my child? What can I do to prevent that?

942. Heal your own childhood wounds.

943. Get a video camera and take tons of family movies.

944. Bake homemade fortune cookies and insert your own fortunes that pertain to your child's interests.

945. Frame a wonderfully whimsical print for your child's room.

946. Encourage your child to remain celibate till he marries.

947. Tour a local historic mansion together and show your child a peek at the grand old days.

948. Read The Night Before Christmas to your child during the holidays.

949. Learn to laugh with your child, not at your child.

950. Take your child to a wax museum on a rainy Saturday afternoon.

951. Sponsor a zoo animal as a family and visit it often.

952. Let your child play with your pots and pans when he is little. Hardly any other items are quite as fascinating to a little one.

953. Give a young child a large-button calculator.

954. Fall madly in love with your mate all over again. It will bring even more happiness to your child's life.

A mother understands
what a child does not say.

Jewish Saying

955. Take your child to an art fair and let her choose an inexpensive masterpiece for her room.

956. Share a two-pack snack cake with your child.

957. Always carefully consider the consequences of your big parenting decisions.

958. Have your own time-out if you become too
    * Tense   * Critical
    * Angry   * Stressed

959. Stop by your child's school on the first day of school to meet his teacher.

960. Offer an incentive for your child to read an impressive number of books.

961. Choose quality godparents for your child.

962. Update your will before the birth of each child.

963. Watch educational television programs with your child.

964. Take your child to see a big Fourth of July fireworks display.

965. Save for your own retirement so that you won't be a burden to your child.

966. Have your child drink eight glasses of water a day.

967. Take a tour of a candy factory and treat your child to a tasty souvenir at the end.

968. When your child has a cold, give him a bottle of jelly beans for a different kind of get-well pill.

969. Send holiday cards and gifts to our servicemen and -women as a family to show your support for our Armed Forces.

970. Handle your child with care.

971. Keep the light of your inner child burning in your own heart.

972. Buy treats from the ice cream truck.

973. Keep a sack filled with little treasures hidden in the back of your closet so you can bring one out as an on-the-spot reward for exceptional behavior.

974. Make a personalized gift of a
     * T-shirt   * Mug   * Gym bag
     * Pencil set * Tote bag   * Sweatshirt

975. Work hard to get tickets to a sold-out event that your child desperately wants to attend.

———————❤———————

Wherever there is a human being,
there is an opportunity for kindness.

Mark Twain

———————❤———————

976. Hold your child's hand during her first airplane trip.

977. Be sure that your child likes your baby-sitter and feels comfortable staying with her.

978. Flash a big smile at your child whenever he does something right.

979. Celebrate positive thinking by having a
Negativity Day once a month where all
family members must pay a small fine for
* Whiney remarks
* Complaints
* Unkind remarks
Use the money that has been collected to
take the family out for a fun evening.

980. Never give violent video games to your child.

981. Have fun family contests, like
* The first person to make his bed gets
a prize
* The first one to finish his chores wins
a prize
* The first one to brush the dog wins
a prize

982. Teach your child to accept and embrace change.

983. Have wintertime fun, like
* Talks in front of the fireplace
* Celebrating holidays
* Playing in the snow

984. Plan some springtime fun, like
    * Planting flowers   * Walks in the park
    * Kite flying   * Spring break trips

985. Have summertime fun, like
    * Vacations   * Family reunions
    * Swimming   * Picnics
    * Drive-in movies

986. Plan some autumn fun, like
    * Hayrides   * Ball games
    * Fall foliage drives * Fall festivals

987. Explain to your child the importance of finishing what he starts.

988. Share a string of licorice.

989. Hold hands and hug a tree.

990. Talk to the animals with your child.

991. Teach your child to give deeply when he gives.

992. Help your child to understand others' feelings.

993. When your child accompanies you on a business trip, make it fun with
    * Nice hotels   * Dining out
    * Room service   * Exercising in the spa
    * Swimming in the hotel's pool

994. Teach your child how to budget her time.

995. Give your child two important things:
    * Roots
    * Wings

996. Carry a beeper so that your child can always reach you.

997. Take your child to an antique toy auction to give a fun glimpse of the past.

998. Make colorful cookies that your child will love by making old-fashioned chocolate chip cookies with M&M's instead of chips.

999. On Memorial Day visit the graves of fallen war heroes and explain their ultimate sacrifice for our country.

1,000. Have your child wear sunglasses to protect his eyes.

1,001. Teach your child to shrug off insults.

1,002. Be patriotic and have fun by setting off your own fireworks on July 4.

1,003. Give your child your old security blanket.

1,004. Teach your child to pray for his enemies.

1,005. Hang wind chimes outside your child's bedroom window.

In this world we must love one another.

Jean de la Fontaine

1,006. Be careful during the holiday season not to plan too many social engagements that you miss out on quality and quantity time with your child.

1,007. Learn how to scan photographs of your child on your computer so that you can proudly send them by E-mail to your distant relatives.

1,008. If your child is overweight, turn yourself into your child's personal fitness trainer.

1,009. Use your good china for breakfast for your family.

1,010. Tell your child of your dreams for her future and see if she likes them. You may find out that your dreams are not hers. Then let go of them.

1,011. Wake your child up with a big smile on your face and start his day off on a cheerful note.

1,012. Give your child the wonderful book *Dogs Never Lie About Love* by Jeffrey Moussaieff Masson. It will increase his love for animals.

1,013. Give your child homemade chicken noodle soup when he has the flu.

1,014. Choose a family meeting place away from your home that all family members can get to and where they can wait for one another in case of a disaster.

1,015. Lie on the grass together and study cloud formations.

1,016. Start a family business that you can pass on to your child.

1,017. Wash your child's hair in rain water.

1,018. Never abandon your child:
  * Emotionally
  * Spiritually
  * Financially

1,019. In a calm and fair manner, try to handle all family emergencies. You won't help the situation if you fall apart. Be strong for your child's sake.

1,020. Encourage your parents to get very involved with your child.

1,021. Create a room for your child where he can surround himself with things that are important to him.

1,022. Send your child to day camp if she doesn't want to go away to overnight camp.

1,023. Do your best to make your home a safe haven for your child.

Kindness is the language
that the deaf can hear
and the blind can see.

Mark Twain

1,024. Become movie stars—make a family video of a day in the life of your family.

1,025. Pass any inheritance coming your way on to your child and create a brighter financial future for him.

1,026. Make a window seat for a cozy family reading spot.

1,027. Play hooky from your chores this weekend and spend the time with your child.

1,028. Set a romantic example for your child by going out with your spouse on Saturday night.

1,029. Find out what programs your child is watching on television and watch each one to check out its content.

1,030. Hide a loving note in the book that your child is reading.

1,031. Develop a good understanding of child psychology.

1,032. Take your child to a Christmas pageant at a nearby church.

1,033. Attend a self-improvement seminar with your child.

1,034. Understand that shyness may be cute in kids, but it is a social barrier. Work with your child to conquer shyness early in his life.

1,035. Keep up with kids' fashions so that you won't be shocked by your child's wardrobe requests.

1,036. Hand your child the comic section of the newspaper to read on the bus ride to school.

1,037. Become an organ donor so that someone else's child might have the gift of life.

1,038. Write out ten goals for yourself on how you can become a better parent.

1,039. Become a volunteer at a Special Olympics event with your child.

1,040. Teach your child about God's amazing love for her.

1,041. Surround your child with optimists that are
  * Family members   * Neighbors
  * Friends   * Your coworkers

1,042. Take your child to different types of museums.

1,043. Walk a spiritual labyrinth with your child.

1,044. Teach your child to safeguard his health.

1,045. If your child is sick and must miss school, buy a get-well card and get his friends and teacher to sign it for him.

1,046. Take your child to church and school bake sales. Kids love to buy yummy treats for a good cause.

1,047. Teach responsible cat and dog ownership by having all family pets spayed or neutered.

———— ♥ ————

Pray for one another.

James 5:16

———— ♥ ————

1,048. Locate fabulous teachers to be your child's tutors.

1,049. Give your child music lessons.

1,050. Teach your child to have a plan when she must tackle a big project and help her to follow it.

1,051. Think about your role of being a parent with
       * Respect   * Pride
       * Joy   * Love

1,052. Look for your child's special gifts and encourage her to develop them.

1,053. Give thanks at breakfast as a family for the day.

1,054. Work with all family members to make your family a huge success. View all members of your family as team players.

1,055. Love your child even when she is unlovable.

1,056. Remember that kids are a *lifetime* commitment.

1,057. Involve your kids in family decisions whenever you can.

1,058. Encourage your child to take the initiative in life and all it has to offer.

1,059. Give your child feedback on his behavior.

1,060. Write thank-you notes to your child when he does an extraordinary job of helping you around the house.

1,061. *Wisely* punish your child when needed.

1,062. Help your child to create a vision for his life that is quite grand.

1,063. Teach your child to step out of her comfort zone so that she will be better able to meet her goals.

1,064. Encourage your child to take pride in his
   * Home   * Country
   * Church   * Family
   * Schoolwork   * Appearance

PARENTING QUESTIONS TO ASK YOURSELF

What bad habits does my child see me continue to practice?

Has my child ever seen me

* Drink too much?
* Become emotionally or physically abusive?
* Use foul language?
* Steal?
* Tell white lies?
* Cheat?
* Take drugs?
* Flirt with someone other than my spouse?

1,065. Stop passive parenting.

1,066. Make sure that both you and your mate have special times alone with your child.

1,067. Find a good baby-sitter or caregiver, by
  * Asking friends and family for
      recommendations
  * Checking with neighbors for references
  * Calling day-care centers for
      recommendations
  * Asking coworkers for referrals

1,068. When your child is talking to you avoid
  interrupting her.

1,069. Get great advice by reading parenting
  magazines.

1,070. Make sure that family meetings are
  * Fun
  * Informative
  * Open to all members regardless of age
  * Not too long in length

1,071. Explain scary events to children.

1,072. Pretend that you are lying on your deathbed and imagine what thoughts you would have about your parenting skills. Try to learn from your insights.

1,073. Be very careful about whom you allow to come into your home. You can never be too cautious.

1,074. Lock your doors when you and your child are riding in your car.

1,075. Teach your child that she is creative. We all are!

1,076. Be friendly with other parents everywhere you go and you'll create your own support network.

1,077. Become your child's hero.

1,078. Share stories of your hero with your child.

1,079. Send supportive mail to your child while he is away at camp.

1,080. Give your child fair warning before he gets into trouble.

1,081. Never be afraid to properly discipline your child.

1,082. Keep your family on your budget to avoid financial problems.

1,083. Be sensitive to children's fears, like
  * Getting lost or being left behind
  * Having to move away from friends
  * Losing a friend
  * Death of a parent or sibling
  * Parents splitting up
  * School violence
  * Not being accepted by peers
  * Making poor grades

1,084. Make a scrapbook of your child's hair-styles and clothing styles. It will be a hoot in years to come.

1,085. Motivate your child.

1,086. Have cute magnets for your refrigerator to hang notes and your child's papers.

1,087. Give your child a gift certificate for an on-line bookstore.

1,088. Create a gingerbread cookie for every member of your family for the holidays.

———————♥———————

To devote a portion of one's leisure
to doing something for someone else
is one of the highest forms
of recreation.

Gerald B. Fitzgerald

———————♥———————

1,089. Don't wait for a crisis to realize how important your child is to you.

1,090. Set seasonal table settings.

1,091. Teach your child that honesty leads to personal freedom and peace of mind.

1,092. When you know it is the wise thing to do, simply mind your own business and let your child make his own decisions.

1,093. Every year on the first day of school, take a picture of your child.

1,094. Explain to your child that other children are looking to her as a role model.

1,095. Never let your child be a bully.

1,096. Ask your child to give you a helping hand during busy times around your house.

1,097. Live a whole life with your child today. Give enough love to last a lifetime.

1,098. Keep a file for your child that includes
* Report cards   * Birthday cards
* Awards   * Artwork
* Mementos   * Ticket stubs
* Doctor's reports

1,099. Never expect parenting to be problem-free. Look for the opportunities that lie in solving those problems.

1,100. Don't leave what your child chooses to think about to chance. Provide stimulating topics for discussion.

1,101. Get your child's input on the little decisions of life, like
* What to have for meals
* Where to go when dining out
* What games to play

1,102. Don't allow your child to put himself down. Stop his negative self-talk.

1,103. Encourage your child to buy a small gift for
* Your spouse   * Grandparents
* Family pet   * His friends
* Your friends

1,104. Tell your child that you will *always* be there for him.

———— ♥ ————

Comparison is a death knell to sibling harmony.

Elizabeth Fishel

———— ♥ ————

1,105. After an argument, hug your child.

1,106. Be a living example of integrity.

1,107. If you can't be with your child when she is home sick, try to get another family member to stay with her, like
* Your spouse
* Grandparents
* Aunt or uncle

1,108. Decorate the outside of your home for holidays.

1,109. Teach your child to respect
* Policemen
* Teachers
* Spiritual Leaders

1,110. Make homemade
* Brownies   * Cookies
* Desserts

1,111. Hold hands while having serious
discussions.

1,112. Teach your child how to use your fire
extinguisher.

1,113. Make sure your family has access to a
good
* Doctor   * Lawyer
* Dentist   * Repairman

1,114. Make sure any coworkers who come to
your home are kind and respectful to your
child.

1,115. Be tactful when speaking with your
child's
* Friends' parents   * Teachers
* Coaches   * Friends
* Day-care workers   * Schoolmates
* Sunday school teachers

1,116. Have a sugary good time; give your child some
  * Rock candy
  * Maple sugar candy

1,117. Insist that your child wear his seat belt when riding with others.

1,118. Write a great inscription in every book that you give to your child.

1,119. Have your child make a donation in the collection basket at church.

1,120. On a cold night, lend your child your jacket or sweater if she doesn't have one.

1,121. When your child is up late doing homework, fix hot cocoa and animal crackers for her.

1,122. Do nice things for your child that he will never know that you did.

1,123. Get to know your neighbors and introduce your child to them.

1,124. Celebrate with the whole family:
  * Birthdays   * Graduations
  * Holidays   * Good report card days
  * Anniversaries

1,125. Keep small children and family pets away from poisonous holly plants and poinsettia.

1,126. Send two bouquets instead of one when you send flowers to your child.

1,127. Spend the longest night of the year (December 21) at a family slumber party.

1,128. Give your child a small gift for all of the twelve days of Christmas and the eight nights of Hanukkah.

1,129. Make homemade greeting cards on your home computer.

Childhood knows
the human heart.

Edgar Allan Poe

1,130. Call your spouse to plan something
together for your child.

1,131. Have a Child Appreciation Day.

1,132. Give your child books about school subjects
that are of particular interest to him.

1,133. Help your child to send out holiday and
birthday cards.

1,134. Have the entire family get together to
decorate the Christmas tree.

1,135. Read the Bible and let your child see you
doing it.

1,136. Demonstrate your talents to your child.

1,137. Patiently answer all of your child's "why" questions.

1,138. Comfort your child through
    * Touch   * Listening
    * Sharing   * Hugging

WAYS TO RELIEVE PARENTING STRESS

* Pray
* Pound a pillow
* Take deep breaths
* Step outside and look up at the big blue sky
* Exercise
* Call a friend
* Go into the bathroom for a little private time
* Visit with your parents

1,139. For moms only—make your child a priority before your

* Career
* Housework
* Social obligations
* Parents
* Girlfriends

1,140. Hide a kind note in a box of junk food. Trust me, your child will find it!

1,141. Give your child your business card to carry in her wallet in case of an emergency.

1,142. If your child is seriously allergic to anything have her wear a medical tag to let others know of her condition.

1,143. When your child is ill and you can't be there, call home to check on her.

1,144. Give your child a copy of your favorite prayer book and write a note telling which prayers mean the most to you and why.

1,145. Eat in your dining room and stop saving it for company.

1,146. Dress so that you won't embarrass your child.

1,147. Buy an antique toy for your child.

1,148. Never take your child for granted.

1,149. Read all of the current parenting best-sellers.

1,150. Help your child to find a good summer job.

1,151. Hide a favorite candy bar in your child's
   * Desk   * Homework
   * Closet

1,152. Give your child a gift certificate for lessons of her choice.

1,153. Have an interdependent family instead of a codependent one.

1,154. Stay up with your child to watch for Santa on December 24.

1,155. Take your child on a Christmas lights tour.

1,156. Ask your child how she can feel
   * Happier   * More appreciated
   * More secure   * Better about herself

1,157. Have a breakfast picnic.

Home is where the heart is.

Anonymous

1,158. Remember that happy homes are
   * Clean   * Peaceful
   * Abuse-free   * Orderly
   * Well maintained

1,159. Teach your child to give sincere compliments for they are spirit lifters that everyone loves to receive.

1,160. Eat dinner with your child in front of your holiday decorations to get into a festive mood.

1,161. Teach your child that there are always consequences to her behavior.

1,162. Send your child to Sunday school.

1,163. Have a weekly Family Fun Night.

1,164. Create your own signals to say "I love you" like
   * A blown kiss
   * A pinkie finger wave
   * A special hand signal
   * A big high five

1,165. Start a family book club.

1,166. Let your small child climb in bed with you on lazy Saturday mornings.

1,167. Cut down your own Christmas tree on a tree farm with your child.

1,168. Go to see your child's every performance in the school play.

1,169. Have a family sing-along.

1,170. Teach your child to be friends with people of all ages.

1,171. On Halloween, tell age-appropriate ghost stories by candlelight.

1,172. Monitor your child's chat room when he is on the Internet.

1,173. Teach your child to meditate.

1,174. Host your child's birthday bash at a trendy restaurant.

1,175. Teach your child to look for the mystical.

PARENTING QUESTIONS TO ASK YOURSELF

What do you think about...
  * God
  * Life
  * Members of the opposite sex
  * Marriage
  * The value of a good education
  * Family members
  * Morals and values
  * Ethics
  * Romance
  * Sex

Beware—your child is looking to you for the answers!

1,176. Teach your child to be kind to strangers. After all, some are angels in disguise.

1,177. Take your child to Disneyland/Disney World.

1,178. Have your child's hearing checked regularly.

1,179. Hunt for four-leaf clovers together.

1,180. Have a fifteen-minute brainstorm session to look for:
* New things to do
* Better ways to run the family
* Settle any outstanding issues.

1,181. When your child is in the sunshine, be sure that he wears a sunscreen to prevent cancer.

1,182. Take your child to see a Broadway show.

1,183. Talk grandparents into making old-fashioned homemade toys for your child.

1,184. Introduce your child to your childhood buddies.

1,185. Attend a church service in your childhood church with your child.

1,186. Have your child learn life saving at your local Red Cross or YMCA.

1,187. Give your child a good encyclopedia for your home computer.

1,188. Tell your child specific reasons why you think he is terrific. It will bolster his self-esteem.

1,189. Take your child Christmas shopping in a big city and let her catch the holiday spirit among the magical sights and sounds of the season.

1,190. Hide snowballs in your freezer and bring them out for some great summertime fun.

1,191. Have a family dinner party and use your
   * Fine china   * Good silverware
   * Crystal   * Table linens

1,192. Tuck an inspiring quote into your child's pocket.

1,193. Meander through antique shops together for a fun lesson in history.

1,194. Read your parents' and grandparents' love letters to your child to teach her about real love, not Hollywood's version of a love affair.

1,195. Take a family vacation every year.

1,196. Stay up to date on kids' culture. Your child will appreciate it.

1,197. After dinner tonight, go bike riding with your child.

1,198. Buy a gallon of your child's favorite ice cream, get two spoons, and have an ice cream attack together.

1,199. Take your child to see the Grand Canyon.

1,200. Treat your child like a human being who is worthy of great respect.

1,201. Rent the movie Pollyanna to teach your child the importance of looking on the bright side of life.

1,202. Try to let your children work out their squabbles between themselves before you intervene.

1,203. Stop emphasizing status symbols to your child.

1,204. Explain to your child that winning isn't everything.

It takes a heap o' livin' in a house t' make it home.

Edgar A. Guest

1,205. Take your child to a candlelight service on special holidays.

1,206. If you move, make sure that your child's friends have his new address.

1,207. Walk out of bad movies with your child.

1,208. Let your child have his own
   * Identity   * Dreams   * Wishes
   * Goals   * Hopes   * Desires
   * Life

1,209. Cut down on the amount of caffeine that your child consumes.

1,210. Monitor your language when your child is around if you are prone to use inappropriate language. Work to stop your bad language habits.

1,211. Be a shining parenting example for all to see.

1,212. Give a special Christmas ornament to your child each year and by the time he leaves home, he will have a nice collection to call his own.

1,213. Encourage your child to read during the summer.

1,214. Teach your child that God has a plan for his life and that nothing happens by accident.

1,215. Linger a little after parent-teacher meetings to become better acquainted with your child's teachers.

1,216. Give a Christmas gift to your child's teacher.

1,217. Inspire your child to experiment, to grow, and to change.

1,218. Never allow any family put-downs.

1,219. Never gossip about members of the family.

1,220. Teach your child to fight through his fears.

1,221. Teach your child to love our great nation by
   * Celebrating the Fourth of July in a big way
   * Reading the Declaration of Independence
   * Singing patriotic songs
   * Visiting historic sights
   * Learning the Pledge of Allegiance
   * Traveling around the country to see its splendor

1,222. Refrain from critiquing your child in public.

1,223. Tell great stories to your child that will teach her to use her power of visualization and imagination.

1,224. Learn from your child. Let her show you the way to go.

1,225. Keep in mind that your child has a right to privacy.

1,226. Teach him to live the life that only he is meant to live.

1,227. Leave your child's previous mistakes in the past.

———————— ♥ ————————

Don't deprive yourself of
the joy of giving.

Michael Greenberg

———————— ♥ ————————

1,228. Learn what age-appropriate behavior is and then stop expecting too much from your child.

1,229. Put these phrases to work for you:
 * I am proud of you
 * Can I help you?
 * What do you think?
 * How do you feel?
 * You are a fabulous person

1,230. Always be approachable.

1,231. Permit your child to fail.

1,232. Keep in mind that your child will only be little for such a short time. Don't waste a single second of it!

1,233. If you are a working mom, give yourself a break from trying to turn every moment with your child into a memorable one. Be realistic.

1,234. Create a home environment that will make your child want to bring his friends home, by
   * Keeping your house neat and tidy
   * Serving snacks
   * Being friendly
   * Allowing for appropriate privacy

1,235. Volunteer as a family on your family's vacation to work for a charity.

1,236. Be your child's
   | * Ally | * Comrade | * Friend |
   | * Chum | * Pal | * Buddy |

   * Parent
   GET THE POINT!

1,237. If you are going to give your child a nick-name, make it a positive, upbeat, and pleasing one.

1,238. Gently prepare your child for the real world. After all, that is one of the most important aspects of being a parent.

1,239. Stop trying to entertain your child every single second of the day.

1,240. Give your child chores to do around your home from an early age.

1,241. Know the basic needs of all children:
    * Food   * Shelter
    * Love   * Religious and moral training
    * Education * Health care
    Be sure to meet those needs.

1,242. Make a big production out of special birthdays like your child's
    * Tenth   * Thirteenth   * Sixteenth

1,243. Have a planning session with your spouse about rule setting for your child.

1,244. Let yourself off the hook if you aren't the perfect parent. Just do your best and make sure that it is enough!

1,245. Understand that bickering between siblings is just part of the package of having more than one child.

1,246. Ask for your child's ideas and opinions. You may get a million-dollar idea!

1,247. Allow yourself extra time to get your family to appointments and engagements. That way you all will feel less stress.

1,248. Teach your child that being a family member is a privilege and should not be taken for granted.

1,249. Inspire your child to make friends with kids who are emotionally well adjusted.

Calmness is always godlike.

Ralph Waldo Emerson

1,250. Teach your child to respect all family members, including distant relatives.

1,251. Keep your promises to your mate. Little ones learn about male/female relationships from watching you.

1,252. Use your sense of humor to
  * Get your point of view across
  * Make family life more enjoyable
  * Be a role model for seeing the bright side of life

1,253. Be sure that your friends are good role models for your child.

1,254. Closely examine the type of role model your parents are for your child.

1,255. Refrain from gossiping with other parents about your kids.

1,256. Understand that your job as a parent includes your role as a
  * Teacher   * Mentor   * Spiritual guide

1,257. Share a cup of hot cocoa at the end of a hard day with your child.

1,258. Open up your child to the wonderful worlds of
   * Art   * Poetry
   * Literature   * Music

1,259. Hide a love note in your child's bath towel.

1,260. At the end of the year write a letter about how much you enjoyed the holidays with your child and hide it in the decorations for her to find the following year.

1,261. Teach your child that she can pray anytime and anywhere.

1,262. Serve a cold lunch on a hot day.

1,263. Give your child a big share of your heart.

1,264. Keep in mind that some of the best things in life to do with your child are still free:
   * Bicycle rides
   * Playing in a park

      * Long walks
      * Talks on the back porch swing
      * Picking wildflowers
      * Playing with the family pet

1,265. Don't take your child for granted. There are thousands of childless couples who would trade places with you in a heartbeat.

1,266. Keep in mind that it is often the smallest gestures of kindness that are remembered the longest.

1,267. Picture in your mind just how much you would miss your child if she wasn't around.

1,268. Take a walk around the neighborhood together when the leaves are turning colors in the fall.

1,269. Teach your child that learning is fun and drive this point home by constantly teaching yourself new skills.

1,270. Make sure that your child gets a little bit of exercise every day.

1,271. Order unusual toys through mail order catalogs.

1,272. Prevent your family's day-to-day life from getting boring.

1,273. Stop complaining about your kids. If there is a problem, solve it and then move on!

PARENTING QUESTIONS TO ASK YOURSELF

* Do my spouse and I provide a safe environment for our child?
* Do my spouse and I set a good example of marriage?
* Is my spouse a good parent?
* What areas of parenting do my spouse and I disagree on?

1,274. Make a huge effort to change your relationship with your child for the better. Just start off by making small, but positive changes. Those little changes will add up over time to great improvements in your relationship.

1,275. Keep in mind that kids go through stages. Relax, take each stage as it comes. Remember this too shall pass.

1,276. Create little rituals to help you relax throughout the day, like
    * Soothing bubble bath
    * Solitary walk
    * Journal writing
    * Drinking herbal tea

1,277. Tell your child fun stories about your parents.

1,278. Keep things in perspective. For example, just because your child gets a bad grade on a test, it doesn't mean that she is going to flunk out of school.

1,279. Refrain from making unflattering remarks about your in-laws in front of your child.

1,280. Help your child to see life as an adventure.

1,281. Stop being an uptight parent. Remember that you chose to be a parent because you thought it would be fun and you would have someone to love. Enjoy it! You got what you wanted.

1,282. Kidnap your child from school to have a special birthday lunch.

1,283. Help your child to find creative ways to earn money.

1,284. Let your dog or cat sleep at the foot of your child's bed. They will both feel safer.

1,285. Take your child to ethnic restaurants to expose him to different cultures.

1,286. Decorate your Christmas tree solely from ornaments and garlands that you and your child have made together.

1,287. Introduce your child to all types of music, including:
* Folk * Jazz * Country
* Classical * Rock * Gospel

1,288. Allow your child to safely explore the world.

1,289. Design a crossword puzzle for your child that expresses your love.

1,290. Post cute cartoons that "hit home" with your child on the refrigerator.

1,291. Declare your love for your child in a happy ad in the classifieds.

1,292. Try to lighten your work load so that you can spend more time at home.

1,293. Sew your child's special occasion clothes and save them as future family heirlooms.

1,294. Prepare your child for the birth of siblings with great empathy and understanding.

1,295. Look for a rainbow with your child and make wishes on it.

1,296. Have a star named for your child.

1,297. Volunteer at a hospice with your child. It will teach her so much about life, death, and compassion.

1,298. Make huge homemade bunnies at Easter for all family members.

1,299. When your child spends a night at a friend's home, tuck a little note in her suitcase saying that you miss her.

1,300. If you suspect that your child or any child is being abused, seek help immediately!

1,301. Have great prizes and favors at your child's birthday party.

1,302. When your child stays over at a friend's home, send along a nice hostess gift for the friend's mother.

1,303. When your child has dinner at a friend's home, have your child take dessert, flowers, or a small gift to the hostess.

1,304. Arrange to have a foreign pen pal for your child.

———————— ♥ ————————

Every baby born into the world is a finer one than the last.

Charles Dickens

———————— ♥ ————————

1,305. Ask your child for a kiss.

1,306. Acknowledge that your child is a living breathing miracle.

1,307. Have the entire family take up yoga to ease stress.

1,308. Don't yell in your home. If you need to talk to someone, walk into the room where she is in order to chat with her.

1,309. Understand that kids act in ways that get them the most attention, regardless of whether it is good or bad attention.

1,310. Never let your child hear you criticize her to grandparents.

1,311. Get the family together earlier so that you can have longer family dinner hours.

1,312. Keep in mind that household rules must be
* Consistent
* Followed by the entire family

1,313. Put your children's needs above your own.

1,314. Prepare your child for the world of dating.

1,315. Use paper place mats and color crayons at the dinner table and have each person create great "art" as well as good conversation.

1,316. Never throw out your child's outgrown toys without checking with him.

1,317. Make sure your child has heard or read Martin Luther King's famous civil rights speech.

1,318. Start a list of all of the things that you wish your child would understand about the world and give it to her on her sixteenth birthday.

1,319. Warn your child about the dangers of burning his bridges.

1,320. Have your child spend time with holy people.

1,321. Take your child to a library book sale.

1,322. Teach your child to seize the moment.

1,323. Turn your child into royalty by taking her to visit a castle.

Do all the good you can.
By all the means you can.
In all the ways you can.
In all the places you can.
At all the times you can.

Anonymous

1,324. Help your child to gracefully end her temper tantrums.

1,325. Buy a gigantic pumpkin to carve for Halloween.

1,326. Teach the joy that comes from helping others.

1,327. Write a fable about your child's life.

1,328. Donate blood when your child is seriously ill.

1,329. Give a WWJD (What would Jesus do?) bracelet to encourage your child to make sound decisions.

1,330. Give the family pet a break from the kids to help keep it from feeling overwhelmed. This will make for a much safer and happier furry friend.

1,331. Encourage your child to join a prayer group.

1,332. Teach your child to be his own true friend.

1,333. Create a family trivia game.

1,334. Keep your child's friends' confidences.

1,335. Keep in mind that good parenting requires good people skills.

1,336. Pass on good family news to your child
regarding
   * Grandparents   * Aunts and uncles
   * Cousins

1,337. Place the responsibility of being a role
model for your child in the forefront of
your mind.

1,338. Know the ten qualities needed for parenting:
   * Sense of humor
   * Compassion
   * Self-control
   * Good self-esteem
   * Wisdom
   * Being a good listener
   * Sense of fun and adventure
   * Spirituality
   * Love
   * Commitment to your child

1,339. Make sure your child knows the house
limits when you aren't there.

1,340. Do a daily family check:
    * Have I had a good conversation with my child?
    * Did we eat at least one meal together?
    * Have we prayed together?
    * Have we hugged?
    * Have we laughed together?

1,341. If you are having serious problems in your marriage, get help. Trust me, it is affecting your child.

1,342. When hiring a baby-sitter, trust your instinct.

1,343. Learn good parenting skills from a trained family counselor.

1,344. Face your parenting fears.

1,345. Network with other parents to get good tips about
    * Teachers   * Schools
    * Kids' programs   * Child care

1,346. If you had a bad childhood, remember that you aren't a prisoner of your past. You can change things for your child.

1,347. Make time for activities that make your child happy.

1,348. Stop doing unnecessary tasks just because you want to be a super parent.

1,349. Point your child in the right direction so that she will have the marketable skills needed to get a summer or part-time job.

In a united family,
happiness springs of itself.

Chinese Proverb

1,350. Teach your child to bake yummy pies and he will always be a welcome guest in others' homes.

1,351. Laugh in the face of family chaos.

1,352. Invite your child's friends over for dessert instead of dinner and it will make life so much easier for you. Plus, your child still has the joy of entertaining her friends.

1,353. Cook dinner with your child. Your child will learn about meal planning and preparation. Plus, you'll get to spend some time together.

1,354. Hang congratulatory signs around the house when your child gets a good report card.

1,355. If your child is sick, don't cause him to worry by the way you react to him.

1,356. Buy colorful, patterned toothbrushes for your child.

1,357. Read Paul Reiser's book Babyhood to put a smile on your lips.

1,358. Each week have a family member give one reason in writing telling what she loves about all other members of the family. Share these uplifting thoughts over Sunday dinner.

1,359. Encourage your child to give outgrown clothing to charity.

1,360. Teach your child that success is a choice, but so is failure. One must be wise to make the right choice.

1,361. If your child wants to be a baby-sitter, make sure that she gets proper training before she starts caring for little ones.

1,362. Point out areas that need improvement in your child's life in a positive, respectful manner.

1,363. Sometimes, give in a little and make a wise compromise with your child.

1,364. Pass on good news to your child about your friends, interests, and job so that he feels more connected to your life.

1,365. When changes are coming in your family like a birth, death, or transfer be sure to talk about the events well in advance with your child.

1,366. Try to get all of the needed resources to help your child to live up to his potential.

———————— ❤ ————————

One should no more be affectionate
in front of a child without including him
than eat in front of him
while he remains hungry.

Eric Berne

———————— ❤ ————————

1,367. Share some cotton candy.

1,368. Strive to be your child's all-time favorite role model.

1,369. Celebrate February 29 as a family in a zany, outrageous manner.

1,370. Try to connect what your child is learning in school to the real world.

1,371. Become your child's confidant.

1,372. Remember when your child is wrong to condemn the bad behavior and not the child.

1,373. When your child is small be sure to respond quickly to her cries.

1,374. Read in front of your child to set an example. Read all kinds of materials to pique his interest in reading, like
    * Books   * Newspapers   * Magazines
    * Letters   * Poetry

1,375. Be decisive when dealing with your child. Understand your own principles, rules, and standards before they are questioned.

1,376. Be wary of sending your child to pre-school too early in life.

1,377. Meet with all of your child's coaches.

1,378. Attend school board meetings when the issues on the agenda will affect your child.

1,379. After a serious discussion, hug your child.

1,380. Refrain from using bribery on your child.

1,381. Ask your child's teacher how you can help your child and how you can help the teacher.

1,382. Bestow upon your mate, in front of your child:
   * Love   * Affection
   * Respect   * Kindness

1,383. Never make fun of your child's feelings. Try to validate them whenever possible.

———— ♥ ————

If we had paid no more attention to
our plants than we have to our children,
we would now be living in a
jungle of weeds.

Luther Burbank

———— ♥ ————

1,384. Advise your child to listen to her inner
voice and to follow its advice.

1,385. Try to turn your child's dreams into reali-
ties.

1,386. Have a mid-afternoon snack together at a
sidewalk café.

1,387. Take your child to a quaint coffee shop for
breakfast.

1,388. Spend at least fifteen minutes of every
day really chatting with your child.

1,389. Buy a good bottle of wine during your
child's birth year and put it away until his
twenty-first birthday. Bring it out for a
wonderful birthday dinner celebration.

1,390. Read *The Little Engine That Could* to your
child to inspire a "can do" attitude.

1,391. Decide who would take care of your child
in case of your death. Work out the
details just in case!

1,392. If your child becomes depressed and stays
that way for two weeks or more, get help
from a professional.

1,393. Create an emotionally supportive environment for the entire family.

1,394. Know the warning signs that something
may be wrong with your child:
   * Changes in friendships
   * Weight gain or weight loss
   * Sudden mood swings
   * Drop in grades

＊Difference in time spent alone
＊Changes in clothing style

1,395. Keep in mind that children are not clones
        of their parents.

1,396. Don't expect or accept disrespectful
        behavior from your child.

1,397. Keep in mind that you shouldn't have
        children if you aren't spiritually,
        emotionally, and financially able to take
        care of them.

AFFIRMATIONS FOR PARENTS

＊I am creative in my role as a parent.
＊I dedicate my life to being a great parent.
＊I always look for the good in my child.
＊I take care of my needs so that I'll be
    able to take care of my child's needs.
＊I am a wonderful parent.

1,398. When a new baby comes into your home, be sure to give extra attention to your other children.

1,399. Search together for little ways to bring happiness and joy into each other's lives.

1,400. Get T-shirt sheets for your child's bed. They are so comfortable!

1,401. Take a steamboat cruise on your next family vacation for some old-fashioned fun.

1,402. Help your child pick out a great gift for your spouse on Mother's Day or Father's Day as the case may be.

Especially for
SINGLE PARENTS

1,403. Watch your dating habits. You are setting examples for your child.

1,404. Remember—no sleepover dates.

1,405. Don't complain about your ex to your child.

1,406. Keep in mind that your child isn't your therapist, so don't run to him with details about your love life.

1,407. Consider your child's feelings about your love life.

1,408. Strive to have a basic understanding of child and adolescent behavior.

1,409. Try to view single parenthood as an adventure instead of a trial.

1,410. Enjoy the freedom you have to do things your way in your parenting role instead of having to compromise with a spouse.

1,411. Hire a baby-sitter to give you a much needed break so that you will appreciate your child even more after a little time away from each other.

PARENTING QUESTIONS TO ASK YOURSELF

* Do I try to give unconditional love to my child?
* When was the last time that I brought a smile to my child's lips?

1,412. Give yourself a little transitional period when you get home from work before you jump right into your role of parenting.

1,413. Accept help from your
   * Ex
   * Parents
   * Child's grandparents on your ex's side
   * Neighbors
   * Friends
   * Church members
   * All former in-laws

1,414. Give yourself a break—your child loves you!
If you're happy, chances are he will be
happy.

1,415. Spend as much time as you can with your
child.

1,416. Don't depend on your child to meet your
social needs. Let your child be a child.

1,417. Have an opposite-sex role model for your
child and make sure that she gets to
spend lots of time with him.

1,418. Ask for help whenever you are over-whelmed.

1,419. Take care of yourself
  * Physically   * Emotionally
  * Spiritually   * Financially
  Your child is depending on you!

1,420. Answer your child's questions regarding her other parent in an age-appropriate manner.

1,421. Think of you and your child as a complete family not a lacking social structure.

1,422. Explain to your child about the many different types of families to reassure him that his type of family is "normal." Talk about
  * Single-parent homes
  * Stepparent homes
  * Adopted-family homes
  * Foster-parent homes

1,423. Accept child support from the other parent.

1,424. Try to encourage your child to get along with your ex.

1,425. Encourage your child to be pleasant to your ex's new spouse or family, if he has remarried.

1,426. Be civil to your child's relatives on your ex's side.

1,427. Try not to be jealous of your child's relationship with your ex.

1,428. Try not to be jealous of your child's relationship with his new stepparent.

1,429. Don't compete with your ex for your child's affection.

1,430. Maintain a healthy respect for members of the opposite sex for your child to see.

There is no friendship, no love
like that of the parent for the child.

Henry Ward Beecher

1,431. Take your child to visit prestigious universities and talk about some of the notable
graduates.

1,432. Allow your child to make a frivolous purchase.

1,433. Be a tutor for a child who needs help and
who is a friend of your child's. Your child
will be so proud of you.

1,434. Don't answer the phone during serious
conversations with your child.

1,435. Blindfold your child and take him to the
surprise outing of his dreams.

1,436. When your child is short of cash, make a money wreath out of dollar bills and hang it on the door to your child's room.

1,437. Write down all of the major events that happen in the life of your family. Give it to your child on a memorable birthday.

1,438. Have a session of laughter with your child that lasts for a long time.

1,439. Read seasonal stories to your child throughout the year.

1,440. Play music loud enough that the whole family can sing along and not feel self-conscious.

1,441. Create a little window box garden if you live in the city, just to grow fresh herbs or flowers for your family.

1,442. Make tape recordings of family holiday sing-alongs. Play the old ones during the entire holiday season.

1,443. Give your child only sugar-free gum.

———————— ♥ ————————

You can learn many things from children.
How much patience you have, for instance.

Franklin P. Jones

———————— ♥ ————————

1,444. Get a library card for you and your child.

1,445. Read to your child all kinds of information
        to teach the value of being able to read
        well. Read
        * Maps
        * Billboards
        * Information shown on television
        * Signs in stores
        * Street signs

1,446. Celebrate Christmas with your family in
        Bethlehem for a once in a lifetime holiday
        event.

1,447. Encourage your child to read the classics.

1,448. Show your child that it isn't good to carry a grudge by your own example.

1,449. Take your child to a foreign land via the Internet, books, and tapes.

1,450. Take your child out to a trendy restaurant to celebrate a good report card.

1,451. Buy a huge piñata for a big birthday cele-bration.

1,452. Stop yourself from pushing your child too hard. Remember that studies show that overachieving kids often tend to burn out along the way.

1,453. Subscribe to a newspaper and encourage your child to read it. He will learn so much about the world this way.

1,454. Play in the first snowfall of the season and create some wonderful memories.

1,455. Teach your child the fine art of being able to make wise, well-thought-out decisions.

1,456. Build a house of cards together on a rainy afternoon. Be sure to take a picture of your mansion.

1,457. Teach your child that sometimes the smartest choice is to break the rules.

1,458. Always answer your child's questions honestly.

1,459. Encourage your child to keep a diary. It will provide a wonderful personal history, plus it will help her to sort out her feelings and thoughts.

1,460. Explore your city together as if you were tourists. Take lots of photos.

1,461. Teach your child to pray with great
  * Expectation
  * Gratitude
  * Faith

1,462. On your child's birthday, let her choose
        the type of cake and ice cream she wants
        for her celebration.

1,463. Help your child to find age-appropriate
        reading material so that reading will be
        more enjoyable for him.

———————— ❤ ————————

Little girls are the nicest things
that happen to people.

Alan Beck

A boy is a magical creature—you can
lock him out of your workshop,
but you can't lock him out
of your heart.

Alan Beck

———————— ❤ ————————

1,464. Give him some Hardy Boys mysteries to read on rainy afternoons.

1,465. Buy matching father/son team shirts to wear to the big game.

1,466. Give your son your old team sweater or jacket.

1,467. Allow him to develop his sensitive side.

1,468. Take him to see the Indianapolis 500 for some fast-paced fun.

1,469. Teach him how to dance.

1,470. Give him your old comic books.

1,471. Present him with your old baseball mitt and glove.

1,472. Have a parent/son breakfast out.

1,473. Give him your old set of toy soldiers.

1,474. Plan a father/son camping trip.

1,475. Teach him to respect girls and women.

1,476. Show him how to do the laundry.

1,477. Take him to the
   * Super Bowl   * World Series
   * NBA finals   * Stanley Cup finals
   * Wimbledon—a jolly good idea!

1,478. Design and build a clubhouse together.

1,479. Take him to see the newest action film.

1,480. Explain to him how stupid and dangerous road rage is.

1,481. Get out your old toys to play with together,
like your
* Train set   * Chemistry set
* Telescope   * Lincoln Logs

---♥---

The heart that loves is always young.

Greek Proverb

---♥---

1,482. Encourage your son to get in touch with
his feelings.

1,483. Teach your son to cook.

1,484. Explain to him that violence doesn't solve
problems, but only creates more troubles.

1,485. Give him a nice quality shaving kit when it
is time for his first shave.

1,486. Buy matching father/son bathrobes.

1,487. Show him how to iron. Beware of burnt fingers and clothing.

1,488. Knit a great-looking ski sweater for him.

1,489. Teach him to be thoughtful and chivalrous. His future spouse will love you for it.

1,490. Show him the proper way to tie a tie.

1,491. Make sure that he spends plenty of time with men who are good role models.

1,492. Shoot baskets together on Saturday mornings.

1,493. Make a handmade teddy bear for him.

1,494. Take him to a Wild West ghost town.

1,495. Build a remote-control car, boat, or plane together.

1,496. Show him ways that he is like his grand-father and father that are positive.

1,497. Build models together and decorate his room with them.

1,498. Give him some great westerns to read and open up a part of our country's history to him.

1,499. Teach him about a man's code of honor.

1,500. Consider giving your son your name at birth.

1,501. Name your son after your
   * Father
   * Grandfather
   * Hero

1,502. Teach him the proper way to lift weights.

1,503. Take him to a baseball spring training camp.

1,504. Browse through an auto show together.

1,505. Take him to a demolition derby.

Love your children with all your hearts,
love them enough to discipline them
before it is too late. . . . Praise them for
important things, even if you have to
stretch it a bit. Praise them a lot. They live
on it like bread and butter and they need it
more than bread and butter.

Lavina Christensen Fugal

1,506. Give him some army fatigues.

1,507. Spend the afternoon at an arcade having
fun together.

1,508. Teach him to do your best card tricks.

1,509. Give him the latest electronic gadget that
has caught his fancy.

1,510. Take him to a hardware store and buy him a good-quality toolbox. Then on holidays, give him a tool. By the time he leaves home, he will have a good collection to build whatever he wants.

1,511. Read biographies of great men to him.

1,512. Take your son white water rafting.

1,513. Get a natural high together. Take him up in a hang glider or sail plane.

1,514. Give him two tickets to see his favorite team play.

Any woman who has a career and a family automatically develops something in the way of two personalities, like two sides of a dollar bill, each different in design. . . . Her problem is to keep one from draining the life from the other.

Ivy Baker Priest

1,515. Help him to build a cool lemonade stand.

1,516. Supersize your junk food lunch and share it with your little buddy.

1,517. Take his team out for pizza or burgers after a big game.

1,518. Help him with his paper route during bad weather.

1,519. Share a large bucket of balls at the driving range.

1,520. Enter the Soap Box Derby together.

1,521. Teach him to skip rocks across a lake.

1,522. Volunteer to be the assistant coach on his T-ball team.

1,523. Take him bumper bowling.

1,524. Make it a tradition to attend the annual YMCA All-You-Can-Eat Pancake Day.

1,525. Teach him to respect the police.

1,526. Spend Saturdays at the batting cages.

1,527. Help him pick out a nice birthday gift for your mate.

1,528. Encourage his participation in spiritual activities.

1,529. Never tease him about the things that are important to him.

1,530. Teach him how to properly oil his new baseball mitt.

1,531. Explain to him what the "infield fly rule" is all about.

1,532. Include him in your Super Bowl party plans.

1,533. Ride the roller coaster with him one more time, even though you are starting to turn green.

1,534. Put up a basketball goal in your backyard.

1,535. Wear matching aprons and chef's hats and let him help you grill out.

1,536. Team up to build the biggest sandcastle of all time.

1,537. Refrain from making it a big deal when you have to get the ladder out again to get the baseball out of the gutter.

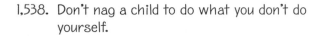

I will act as if I make a difference.

William James

1,538. Don't nag a child to do what you don't do yourself.

1,539. Teach your child that some of the finest things in life are free:
* Love
* Faith
* Happiness
* Health

1,540. Want to spend more time with your child? Consider
* Flex-time work
* Job sharing
* Consulting work
* Working out of your home
* Part-time work
* Being a full-time parent

1,541. Ask your child what he is giving to others for Christmas to put the focus where it should be—on the real meaning of Christmas.

1,542. Have your child slow down when he eats and chew his food slowly. It is good for digestion and encourages a child not to overeat.

1,543. Encourage your children to find special ways to entertain each other.

1,544. Consider having a birthday breakfast for younger kids instead of an afternoon or evening party. The kids will be fresher.

1,545. Never allow a child to spend more than you can comfortably afford.

1,546. Enroll your child in a summer reading program.

1,547. Have a reasonable curfew on weeknights and weekends.

1,548. Provide proper supervision for your child after school.

1,549. Make sure your child gets at least eight hours of sleep per night.

1,550. If you are having a family crisis at home, consider explaining the situation to your child's teacher to get your child some extra emotional support.

1,551. Try to buy toys that are well made and will be able to stand up to many hours of play.

1,552. Give toys that match your child's
 * Personality   * Interests
 * Skill level

1,553. Appreciate the differences between
 * You and your child
 * Your spouse and your child
 * All of your children

1,554. If you have twins or triplets, refer to each child by name and not as "the twins" or "the triplets" for it doesn't acknowledge their individual personalities.

1,555. Refrain from burdening your child with adult problems and situations.

1,556. Take your child on a ride in a helicopter. It will be a thrill for both of you.

1,557. Travel to any towns, cities, or burghs that have your child's first, middle or last name in them. Yes, my husband, Dale, still enjoys a drive through Dale, Indiana.

1,558. Plan a fabulous family trip to an exotic location that none of you has ever been to before. It will make the trip much more exciting for all of you.

1,559. When your spouse is out of town on a business trip, have your child call and say good night to him.

1,560. Inspire your child to be himself and not carbon copies of you and your mate.

1,561. Get rid of the awful notion that children are to be seen but not heard. It is harmful to your child's self-esteem.

1,562. Never underestimate the power of your child's peers.

1,563. Tell two bedtime stories to your child tonight instead of just one.

1,564. Give a variety of Pez dispensers and candy for an inexpensive but fun collection.

1,565. Keep on top of your child's health insurance claims.

1,566. Spend a family vacation on Cape Cod. It is so picturesque.

MAJOR OOPS LIST

Ask yourself if you have made any of these mistakes:

* Broken promises
* Forgotten birthdays
* Been late to pick up your child
* Shamed her
* Revealed your child's secret
* Embarrassed her

1,567. Build a fantastic swing set or play station for your child.

1,568. Never let anyone mistreat your child.

1,569. Grow a fruit tree in the backyard so that your child can eat fresh, homegrown fruit.

1,570. Plan your golden years so that you won't be a burden to your child.

1,571. Have an answering machine so that your child won't miss calls from his friends.

1,572. Take your child to see
   * Windmills
   * Covered bridges
   * Lighthouses

1,573. Cut down on the amount of red meat that your family consumes.

1,574. Take your child to visit the homes of any presidents who have lived nearby.

1,575. Teach your child to stand up for himself and not to have a victim mentality.

1,576. Take your child to see the seven natural wonders of the world.

1,577. Plan lots of fun activities for your child's school breaks.

1,578. Take a religious pilgrimage as a family.

1,579. Put reflectors on the clothes your child wears at night.

1,580. Teach your child to respect all people:
    * Young and old
    * Rich and poor
    * Healthy and sick
    * Black and white
    * Americans and foreigners
    Absolutely everyone!

1,581. Teach your child the skills needed to be a leader.

1,582. Listen closely when your child gives you hints about what she wants for Christmas or her birthday.

1,583. Teach your child how to be a team player.

1,584. Walk along the Riverwalk in San Antonio, Texas. It is so beautiful and your child will love it.

1,585. Give your child the VIP treatment.

PARENTING QUESTIONS TO ASK YOURSELF

* Do I play favorites among my children?
* Do I treat my child consistently or am I sporadic in my parenting?
* Does my child feel loved?
* Does my child feel safe in our home?
* Does my child feel special?

1,586. Walk arm and arm.

1,587. Dress appropriately for parent-teacher conferences.

1,588. Donate books to your child's school library.

1,589. Encourage your child to do extra-credit projects.

1,590. Teach your child that if he doesn't have something good to say, it is often best to remain silent.

1,591. Hide a little note in your child's clothes before storing them away for the season.

1,592. Teach your child not to be intimidated by those with
    * More power
    * More money
    * Higher education

1,593. Hold hands during scary movies.

1,594. Help your child to overcome his fears.

1,595. At Thanksgiving dinner request all family members to say a small grace for what they are most grateful for this year.

1,596. If your child becomes sick with an unusual illness, research all of the possible treatments that are currently available.

1,597. Teach your child to work to save endangered species.

1,598. Inspire your child to work toward saving our planet. After all, it is a really nice place to call home.

1,599. Put in a backyard hot tub for the whole family to enjoy.

1,600. Celebrate your pet's birthday with a family party complete with cake, ice cream, and gifts. Be sure not to feed your dog any chocolate for it can be fatal.

1,601. Listen closely to your child at times when she is most likely to reveal herself, like
* Bedtime
* On the ride to school
* On the ride home from school
* During a walk

1,602. Include grandparents at some family meetings.

1,603. Foster empathy in your child.

1,604. Throw a spur-of-the-moment party.

1,605. When your child is older, ask her what rules she feels are important to live by. Listen and learn.

———————— ♥ ————————

As we read the school reports on our children, we realize a sense of relief that can rise to delight that—thank Heaven—nobody is reporting in this fashion on us.

J. B. Priestley

———————— ♥ ————————

1,606. If you aren't sure about your child's request, give yourself time to think it over before giving him your answer.

1,607. Choose your battles with your child. Don't fight over every little thing!

1,608. Never allow your child to be around anyone who is drinking too much or is doing drugs.

1,609. When your child spends the night at a friend's home, always reassure her that you will come and get her if a problem arises.

1,610. Teach your child to keep her promises to you and your mate.

1,611. If your child is getting to you, take a mental mini-vacation to help yourself unwind.

1,612. Know the parental trouble signs:
    * Hostility toward your child
    * Indigestion
    * Trouble sleeping
    * Poor judgments
    * Depression
    * Mood swings
    * Anxiety
    Get help if you are experiencing serious parental problems. Your child will be glad that you did!

1,613. Deliver food baskets to needy families with your child.

1,614. Take the time needed to make wise, informed plans regarding your child's future.

1,615. Teach your child to gratefully receive God's many blessings.

1,616. Have an Advent calendar complete with little gifts for your child.

1,617. In family disagreements, stick with the present issues and don't bring up the past.

1,618. Get more storage to help you deal with all of the stuff that your kids have, like:
   * Under the bed containers   * Baskets
   * Bookshelves   * Toy box
   * Egg crate storage units

1,619. Take your child to the only mall in America designed just for kids in Grand Rapids, Michigan.

1,620. Take photos of your child regularly, not just on special occasions.

1,621. Teach your child to appreciate life, for it is so fabulous!

1,622. On your child's birthday send a little note telling of all of the joy she has brought into your life.

1,623. Teach your child about credit and debt and how to be a wise consumer.

MAKE BUSINESS TRIPS EASIER ON YOUR CHILD BY

* Explaining why you must go
* Telling all about where you are going
* Showing your destination on a map
* Leaving a number where you can be reached
* Sending a postcard from the hotel where you are staying
* Calling every evening
* Bringing your child a small gift
* Reassuring him of your love before, during, and after the trip

1,624. Remember that your time is more valuable to your child than your money.

1,625. Give a cute piggy bank to your child to encourage her to save money.

1,626. Get your spouse's input on planning your child's extracurricular activities. Two heads are better than one when creating balance in your child's life.

1,627. Refrain from teaching your child to clean his plate at each meal for it leads to obesity.

1,628. Wear accessories that your child would enjoy seeing, like
    * Fun T-shirts   * Cute jewelry
    * Interesting ties   * Novelty scarves

1,629. Look for little ways to improve your child's life.

1,630. Teach your child to make the most of his study time.

1,631. If your child is having serious problems of any kind, seek help from professionals, not just well-meaning family members and friends.

1,632. Treat your child to a surprise the next time you go shopping together.

1,633. When your child is sick, bring home dinner from his favorite restaurant.

1,634. Bring home books, CDs, and movies from the library that you know your child will enjoy.

1,635. When you get an award or promotion, be sure to acknowledge the role your family has played in your accomplishment.

1,636. Create a get-well crossword puzzle for a bedridden child.

1,637. Choose a song for you and your child to have as your theme. Think of each other every time you hear it.

1,638. Have old-fashioned values and teach them to your child.

1,639. Always welcome your child with open arms.

1,640. Send lots of mail to your child when he is away at camp.

1,641. Ask your child's school choir to sing at your Christmas party.

To maintain a joyful family requires much from both the parents and the children. Each member of the family has to become, in a special way, the servant of the others.

Pope John Paul II

1,642. Take your child to dinner with you and your spouse to celebrate your wedding anniversary.

1,643. Make your son "King for a day."
Make your daughter "Queen for a day."

1,644. Make a family chore chart and teach
organization. Include big and little chores,
like
* Empty dishwasher * Vacuum
* Dust   * Prepare meal
* Laundry   * Mow the lawn
* Do dishes

1,645. Get a personalized license plate for his
bicycle or tricycle.

1,646. Design a special holiday decoration for
each of your children.

1,647. Always take your child's telephone call
when you are at work.

1,648. Meet your child at the door when he gets
home from school with a big plate of
cookies.

1,649. Validate your child's feelings whenever you can.

1,650. Take your child out for dinner on her birthday and have a birthday cake served for dessert.

1,651. Shop for little gifts all year long for extra-special holiday and birthday celebrations.

1,652. Encourage your child's grandparents to give your child
* Love   * Time
* Understanding   * Respect

1,653. Take an afternoon trip to a nearby town for a mini-getaway.

1,654. Ask your child's friends what gifts your child would like to receive for his birthday.

1,655. Ask your child to supply you with a list of her favorite meals and desserts and incorporate them into your menu planning.

———— ♥ ————

The most important thing a father
can do for his children is to love
their mother.

Theodore M. Hesburgh

———— ♥ ————

1,656. Decorate an Easter tree together.

1,657. Gladly make sacrifices for your child.

1,658. Try to enjoy all the stages of your child's
life.

1,659. Rent a commercial sign for the front yard
to express
  * Your love
  * Your pride in a specific achievement
  * Birthday greetings
  * Get well wishes

Especially for
GIRLS

1,660. Have a tea party and invite her teddy bears and dolls.

1,661. Play dress-up with your daughter.

1,662. Treat her to a manicure.

1,663. Bake cookies together.

1,664. Encourage her to play sports.

1,665. Take her to your office and/or your spouse's office.

1,666. Play Barbies with her till she tires out, not till you want to quit.

1,667. Read the Nancy Drew mysteries together.

1,668. Buy matching mother/daughter outfits.

1,669. Give her your old doll collection.

1,670. Teach her self-respect and to be proud of her gender.

1,671. Treat her to having her hair styled at a fine salon.

1,672. Start a charm bracelet for her and give charms that relate to
* Holiday destinations
* Hobbies
* Achievements

1,673. Buy her a magical party dress.

1,674. Have lots of pretty bows for her hair.

1,675. Start a china pattern collection of her choice and add a piece to it on all holidays. By the time she leaves home, she will have a wonderful service for at least eight people plus serving pieces.

1,676. Read to her the stories of famous, strong women.

1,677. Give her a beautiful crown to make her feel like a princess.

1,678. Be sure your daughter has a dad/daughter night out on the town on a regular basis.

1,679. Give her a beautiful, feminine robe and nightgown set to make her feel glamorous.

PARENTING QUESTIONS TO ASK YOURSELF

* When you were young, what kind of
  parent did you dream that you would be?
* Are you like that now?
* How do you want to be remembered by
  your children?

1,680. Treat her to a fun makeover at the mall.

1,681. Send her flowers for graduation from
  * Kindergarten
  * Eighth grade
  * High school

1,682. Tie a pretty flower in her hair.

1,683. Start an add-a-bead or add-a-pearl
  necklace for her.

1,684. Give her something with lace on it, like
* Socks   * Ribbons   * T-shirts
* Gloves   * Dress

1,685. Listen to her fashion advice to you.

1,686. Refer to her as your best girlfriend from time to time.

1,687. Send her a May Day bouquet.

1,688. Teach her to be the best athlete in your neighborhood.

1,689. Surprise her with a new necklace and hang it on her doorknob for her to find when she wakes up in the morning.

1,690. Give her modeling lessons to increase her confidence.

1,691. Let her try on your
* Wedding gown   * Evening gowns
* Old bridesmaid dresses

1,692. Encourage her career aspirations.

---💛---

You don't choose your family.
They are God's gift to you,
as you are to them.

Desmond Tutu

---💛---

1,693. Start a collection of Limoges boxes and
add to it on all holidays. Buy boxes that
reflect her interests and travels. It will
make a wonderful way to tell her life story.

1,694. Buy matching mother/daughter Vera
Bradley handbags.

1,695. Teach her some basic self-defense lessons.

1,696. Give her a subscription to *Teddy Bear and Friends* magazine.

1,697. Take her to see a ballet.

1,698. Give her a set of Mary Engelbreit paper dolls to play with or to frame for her room.

1,699. Take her to visit the wonderful dollhouse museums in
* Kansas City, Missouri
* Carmel, Indiana

1,700. Send her a subscription to *Seventeen* magazine.

1,701. Tell her stories about the brave women who are your ancestors.

1,702. Help her to pick out an outstanding Easter bonnet.

1,703. Present her with a locket that contains a picture of
* Jesus
* You and your spouse
* Her beloved four-legged friend
* Her siblings
* Her best friend

1,704. Teach her that frogs are never princes.

1,705. Go shopping together at an antique store to find a special keepsake to treasure for generations.

PARENTING QUESTIONS TO ASK YOURSELF

* When was the last time that my family participated in a family tradition?
* When was the last time that my child had a friend over to play?

1,706. Design and sew her wedding gown.

1,707. Give her your wedding gown to wear when she gets married.

1,708. Present her with her grandmother's
   * Doll   * Ring   * Brooch
   * China   * Comb and brush set

1,709. Knit a darling ski sweater for her.

1,710. Make a homemade doll for her.

Our children are here to stay,
but our babies and toddlers and
preschoolers are gone as fast as they
can grow up—and we have only a
short moment with each.

St. Clair Adams Sullivan

1,711. Send her to finishing school in Paris.

1,712. Take her to see an ice skating show.

1,713. Hide sachets in her drawers.

1,714. Bring a bouquet of flowers to her after
her big recital.

1,715. Host a slumber party for your daughter and her buddies.

1,716. Give her a facial.

1,717. Take a cooking class together.

1,718. Allow her to order a new outfit from a mail order catalog.

1,719. Let her fix your hair.

1,720. Invite her along when you go shopping for clothes.

1,721. Show her how to use makeup.

Misery is when grown-ups don't realize how miserable kids can feel.

Suzanne Heller

1,722. Treat her to a pedicure.

1,723. Give her a piece of gold jewelry on her
  * Tenth birthday
  * Thirteenth birthday
  * Sixteenth birthday
  * Eighteenth birthday
  * Twenty-first birthday

1,724. Buy some cosmetics made especially for
  little girls and give them to her when her
  self-esteem is suffering a bit.

1,725. Let her wear your old
  * Majorette costume
  * Cheerleader uniform
  * Team jersey

1,726. Give her the key to your jewelry box and
  let her enjoy your treasures.

1,727. Get her a doll that resembles her from
  the American Girl Collection.

1,728. Give her a copy of Little Women.

1,729. Let her spend her birthday at a spa.

1,730. Teach her not to be obsessed about her weight.

1,731. Give her a Raggedy Ann doll—the only doll with a heart.

1,732. Take her shopping at a whimsical Mary Engelbreit store.

1,733. Host an all-female relative party for her.

1,734. Give her sound dating advice.

1,735. Present her with a wonderful-smelling bottle of bubble bath.

1,736. Treat her to some cologne made especially for a young woman.

1,737. Give her a pretty cloth apron when she starts to enjoy cooking.

1,738. Let her try on your engagement ring.

1,739. Allow her to borrow your heirloom jewelry for a special occasion.

1,740. Teach her to sew and give her a darling little sewing basket on the day of her first sewing lesson.

1,741. Give her a hope chest on her sixteenth birthday.

PARENTING QUESTIONS TO ASK YOURSELF

* Am I stressing the importance of good, moral character?
* Do I base my parenting decisions on what I know to be right or on what will make me popular with children?
* Do I understand that I am one of the most important teachers and role models in my child's life?
* Am I a good parent? How can I be even better?
* Am I teaching my child great spiritual and religious truths?

1,742. Line her drawers with scented papers.

1,743. Give her a diary that has a lock and key. Don't snoop!

1,744. Help her to understand that Prince Charming exists only in fairy tales.

1,745. Give her a special bookmark to encourage reading.

1,746. Encourage her to demand respect from men and boys.

1,747. Teach her to twirl a baton.

1,748. Present her with a tiny bottle of Chanel No. 5.

1,749. Give her a small bottle of fragrant hand lotion.

1,750. Sew pretty, extra-special buttons on her clothes.

1,751. Give her a heart charm on a necklace as a symbol of your love for her.

1,752. Buy a four-poster bed for her room.

1,753. Collect dolls from all over the world for her.

1,754. Take her to a flower show.

1,755. Give her a perm if she wants curly hair.

1,756. Name your daughter after your
* Mother
* Grandmother
* Sister
* Heroine
* Best female friend

1,757. Compliment her cooking.

1,758. Treat her to a life-sized doll.

1,759. Keep in mind that a doll isn't just a doll, but your daughter's dear friend or baby. Show respect for her special pal.

1,760. Let her put on a mini fashion show when she gets her back-to-school clothes.

1,761. Buy matching mother/daughter robes.

1,762. Treat her to a small Coach handbag.

1,763. Give her a sterling silver
     * Bracelet   * Ring
     * Necklace   * Baby cup
     * Rattle   * Picture frame

1,764. Send her to Dollhouse Creating Camp at Cincinnati Country Day in Indian Hill, Ohio.

1,765. Teach her to do counted cross-stitch.

1,766. Thrill her with a tiny diamond necklace.

1,767. Teach her to knit and crochet.

1,768. Instruct her to ask for what she wants in life and to speak up for herself.

The child is father of the man.

William Wordsworth

1,769. Take her to a fashion show.

1,770. Give her an oyster with a pearl in it for a little surprise.

1,771. Browse through a beautiful clothing boutique together.

1,772. Take her to eat at a restaurant where ladies who lunch dine.

1,773. Visit a castle in England together if she loves the stories of kings and queens.

1,774. Inspire her to want to be the first woman president of the United States.

1,775. Help her to like what she sees when she looks in the mirror.

1,776. Encourage her love of animals by giving her horseback riding lessons.

1,777. Give her a pretty lace hankie when she is brokenhearted and in need of a good cry.

1,778. Help her to see the fun in just window shopping.

1,779. Teach her that men and women are equal.

1,780. Update her hairstyle regularly.

1,781. Place a bunch of flowers in front of her door to find when she gets up in the morning.

1,782. Advise her when she goes to buy her new swimsuit as to what is appropriate for her to wear in public.

1,783. Give her cute stickers for her stationery.

1,784. Treat her to an expensive tube of lipstick in an age-appropriate color.

1,785. Sew her first communion dress.

1,786. Design her christening gown.

1,787. Take her to watch her favorite team play and grab a bite to eat after the game.

1,788. Give her a pretty billfold and tuck a ten dollar bill inside of it.

———————— ♥ ————————

Parenthood remains the greatest single
preserve of the amateur.

Alvin Taffler

———————— ♥ ————————

1,789. Buy cute pillowcases for your child's bed.

1,790. Send your child a congratulatory card
when he accomplishes his goal.

1,791. Never talk about one child to another child
in a gossipy manner.

1,792. Take action if you aren't happy with your
child's
  * Teacher
  * Coach
  * School

1,793. Pretend to thoroughly enjoy your child's
favorite movie every time that you must
suffer through it with him.

1,794. Take your child to see Santa at Holiday World in Santa Claus, Indiana. It is the next best place to the North Pole for a visit with Santa.

1,795. Help your child to throw a party for her grandparents on
* Their wedding anniversary
* Grandparents' Day
* A special birthday

1,796. Help your child to learn a few choice phrases in the languages of his ancestors.

1,797. Give your child a secret decoder ring and write self-esteem affirming messages for him to decipher.

1,798. Allow your child to have angry feelings and teach him how to deal with them in an appropriate manner.

1,799. Have your child take lessons to make the wintertime more fun and safe, like:
* Skiing lessons
* Ice skating lessons

1,800. Take your child to a music festival.

1,801. Introduce your child to the stock market by giving her stock for her birthday; watch it grow together.

1,802. Celebrate together with nonalcoholic beverages.

1,803. Encourage your child to participate in local talent shows.

―――――― ♥ ――――――

It is more blessed to give
than to receive.

Acts 20:35

―――――― ♥ ――――――

1,804. When you have a baby-sitter taking care of your child, be sure that she knows how to reach you in an emergency.

1,805. Arrange to have your child taken for a ride in a classic car.

1,806. Take your child to all local parades no matter how silly they are.

1,807. Take your child to see a local courtroom in action.

1,808. Go through your old scrapbooks with your child and tell him all about your childhood.

1,809. Pick flowers together to use as table decorations at dinner tonight.

1,810. Read the fabulous book Guess How Much I Love You to your child.

1,811. Learn how to install your child's car seat properly. Eighty percent of car seats in the United States are improperly installed.

1,812. Don't give orders to your child as if you are a general: be polite.

1,813. Be wary of health food store supplements that many athletes are taking to improve their bodies for sports. Talk to your doctor before using them.

1,814. Expect rough waters to come from time to time. Be prepared in your role as a parent.

1,815. Work out the type of discipline that you and your spouse will use with your children in advance. Make sure that you both are in agreement.

1,816. If you work the night shift, make an extra effort to get to spend lots of time with your child.

1,817. When you leave your child with a sitter, be honest about your child's good and bad behavior so that she will know what to expect.

1,818. Teach siblings to support, love, and look out for each other.

1,819. Create an environment in your home where all topics can be openly discussed.

1,820. Give your child lots of time with
* Aunts   * Uncles
* Grandparents   * Cousins
Even if you must travel to do it!

1,821. Attend family reunions on both sides of your family.

1,822. Relate to your child in an age-appropriate manner.

1,823. Refrain from saying, "I told you so." Nobody wants or likes to hear it.

1,824. Participate with other families in fun activities.

1,825. Take your child to a dog show.

1,826. Search for ways to feel connected to your
        child.

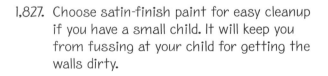

WAYS TO BE A
FABULOUS GRANDPARENT

✳ Love your grandchildren unconditionally
✳ Allow the parents to set the rules and
  adhere to them
✳ Treat all grandchildren equally
✳ Treat all grandchildren as individuals
✳ Be fun
✳ Show your love in a variety of ways
✳ Express your love freely and often
✳ Look for activities that you and your
  grandchild can both enjoy.

1,827. Choose satin-finish paint for easy cleanup
        if you have a small child. It will keep you
        from fussing at your child for getting the
        walls dirty.

1,828. Head for a weekend getaway in the mountains with your child. Being in peaceful, natural surroundings will do a world of good for your relationship.

1,829. Encourage your child to keep his school locker in an orderly fashion. It will make it easier to find things and to keep books and papers neat, and it will help him to understand the importance of a clutter-free environment.

1,830. Tweak your parenting skills even if you are the world's best parent.

1,831. Give your child little coupons, like:
  * Lunch with Mom
  * Movie with Dad
  * Game with Mom and Dad
  * Reading with Dad
  * Shopping with Mom
  * Dinner with parents at a favorite restaurant
  * Hug from Mom
  * Trip to grandparents' house

1,832. Refrain from being overly "helpful" by overlooking irrelevant mistakes.

1,833. Learn the art of napkin folding and create fun works of art for the dinner table that your child will just love to see at his place.

1,834. Send mail to your child and use his nickname or a fun name on the address.

1,835. Have a compliment jar for your child that he can refer to again and again. Simply write out at least twenty-five good things about your child and put them in a specially designated container that he can find whenever he needs a little bit of cheering up.

1,836. When you pray, let your child chime in.

1,837. Be very careful about placing huge demands on your child. Remember he is still just a kid!

1,838. Refrain from having adult conversations in front of your child.

1,839. Start a nice collection for your child, like:
* Ornaments
* Antique toys
* Teddy bears
* Dolls
* Classic books

1,840. Give your child a trophy for being the Number 1 kid in America.

1,841. Frolic in a neighborhood swimming pool together.

1,842. Have a box lunch on the front porch together.

1,843. Send a musical greeting card.

1,844. Buy a book written especially for your child with his name in the story. You can get these made at your local mall or most bookstores.

PARENTING QUESTIONS TO ASK YOURSELF

* Do I pray to be a great parent?
* Do I pray for my child?
* Do my child and I regularly pray together?
* Do I send my child to Sunday school?
* Does my family attend church each week?

1,845. Take your child on a shopping spree in a
    * Bakery   * Candy store
    * Dollar store

1,846. Invite all of the neighborhood kids over for a party no matter their ages and let them get to know one another.

1,847. Host a class reunion of your child's nursery school.

1,848. Check with all of the major hotel chains to learn of their special getaway packages for families.

1,849. Have a little tailgate party when your child gets out of school.

1,850. Make a game of
   * Chores   * Homework
   * Running errands
   Be creative!

1,851. Buy a first edition copy of a great new kid's book for your child.

1,852. Warm your child's bath towel on cold days.

1,853. Place confetti in the greeting cards that you mail to your child.

1,854. Shop party supply stores for fun little trinkets to use for
   * Gifts   * Table decorations
   * Party favors   * Rewards
   * Seasonal decorations

1,855. Enter a contest together.

1,856. Proudly display your child's
   * Awards   * Ribbons
   * Trophies   * Good grades
   * School projects

1,857. Cheer for your child from the sidelines.

1,858. Wear your child's team logo or colors to
   show your support at his functions.

1,859. Teach your child to avoid eye contact with
   strangers when she is out walking alone.

1,860. Send your child an invitation to a family
   event through the mail.

1,861. Stay up all night together to
   * Chat   * Play games
   * Read   * Watch good movies

1,862. Place a comfortable chair in your child's
   room.

1,863. Let your child know that you think about him even when you aren't together.

1,864. When it comes to gift giving for your child, think safety first.

HOW TO HELP KIDS MOVE

* Talk in depth about all aspects of moving
* Hug your child even more than usual
* Let your child share her concerns with you
* Explain that lots of kids move
* Take a trip to your new location before the actual move
* Get your child involved in the moving process
* Try to introduce your child to kids in your new neighborhood before the move
* Invite old friends to your new home
* Make sure your child gets to stay in touch with old friends
* Spend more time with your child
* Get your child's input on decorating her new room

1,865. When you travel with your child, be sure to childproof your hotel room.

1,866. Choose fabrics that wear well on furniture so that your child can be comfortable sitting on your sofa and chairs.

1,867. Give your child a trip diary before he goes on a big vacation.

1,868. Present your child with a one-time-use camera before he goes to camp.

1,869. Give your child a monogrammed key chain when she turns sixteen and gets the keys to the family car or a car of her own.

1,870. Present your child with a spiritual charm or pendant on the next religious holiday.

1,871. Buy a travel guide book before a big family vacation and let the entire family study up on your destination. Let all family members decide what sights to see.

1,872. Send out birth or adoption announcements for your child's arrival. Let the whole world know about your fabulously good news!

1,873. Save the newspaper announcement of your child's birth.

1,874. Have your child christened or baptized.

1,875. Protect your child's
     * Health   * Property
     * Peace of mind   * Home

1,876. Teach your child from an early age to obey the rules.

1,877. Refrain from overdressing your child. Remember it is always more stylish to be underdressed than overdressed.

1,878. Insist that your whole family be neat and tidy when you sit down for a meal.

1,879. Need more time? Get up thirty minutes earlier so that you will be more patient with your child and less rushed.

1,880. Make small gestures of kindness to your child throughout each and every day.

1,881. Teach your child the basics of good table manners to make meals more pleasant for everyone. Teach your child that
* She must be polite during the entire meal
* She must use the utensils properly
* She must ask to be excused when she is finished
* She must chew her food with her mouth closed
* She must not act too silly

1,882. Buy things made especially for left handers if your child is a southpaw.

1,883. Use fun rubber stamps to decorate your child's
* Letters   * Cards
* Schoolwork

1,884. Hold a sign that expresses your love for your child and have your photo taken with it.

1,885. Put a good reading lamp in your child's room.

1,886. When you can't have dinner with your child, get together for lunch.

1,887. Track down any of your old toys that you can find to give to your child; try looking for them at
* Your parents' home
* In the attic
* Your siblings' homes
* Your grandparents' home

———— ♥ ————

You don't raise heroes, you raise sons. And if you treat them like sons, they'll turn out to be heroes, even if it's just in your eyes.

Walter M. Schirra, Sr.

———— ♥ ————

1,888. Win a neat prize for your child at an amusement park or carnival.

1,889. Make an interest-free loan to your child when her funds are low and she has something that she desperately wants to buy.

1,890. Place decorations for each holiday in your child's room.

1,891. "Borrow" grandparents from a close friend if your child doesn't have any so that he can enjoy the company of his elders.

1,892. If you have parenting questions and you want a straight answer call the popular radio talk show host Dr. Laura Schlessinger at 1-800-Dr-Laura.

1,893. On a day that you know will be really tough for him, plan a special surprise activity for your child when he gets out of school.

1,894. Frame fun cartoons that relate to your family.

1,895. Dress nicely when your child entertains her friends in your home.

1,896. Understand that your child is not a mind reader.

1,897. Frame menus from restaurants where your family has shared a special meal.

1,898. Keep your parents up to date on current child safety practices if they baby-sit for your child.

1,899. Share with your spouse your parenting
  * Fears   * Shortcomings
  * Mistakes
  You will feel so much better and, therefore, be a better parent.

1,900. Place party favors for your child at the dinner table tonight to turn the meal into a little festive occasion.

1,901. Frame childhood treasures in a shadow box for your child to keep for a lifetime. Frame
  * Paper dolls   * Baby shoes
  * Small stuffed toys   * Tiny dolls
  * Baby jewelry   * Doll clothes
  * Cars and trucks   * Rattles and crib toys

1,902. Listen to parenting advice from your mother-in-law. She obviously did something right, for you fell in love with her child.

1,903. Start a family band.

1,904. Fly holiday flags for a festive outdoor celebration.

PARENTING QUESTIONS TO ASK YOURSELF

* What are five ways that I could Improve my relationship with my child?
* What is keeping me from doing them?
* How could I arrange to spend more time with my child?
* Do I take my child for granted?
* What should I be doing for my child that I am not currently doing?

1,905. Read the newspaper for articles on child health care issues that will be helpful to your child.

1,906. Go for a ride together in a horse-drawn carriage.

1,907. Host a "This Is Your Life" party for your child.

1,908. Plan fun theme meals for your family, like
* Mexican fiesta   * Chinese cuisine
* Italian pasta   * Hawaiian luau
* All-American picnic   * French cuisine

1,909. Save time in the morning by serving breakfast sandwiches.

1,910. Strive to be successful in all areas of your life so that you can show your child the way.

1,911. Frame great quotes about
* Parenting   * Children
* God's love   * Family ties

1,912. Teach your child that she has God as her Heavenly Father.

1,913. Understand that there are no substitutes for parents, not even
* Grandparents   * Aunts and uncles
* Teachers   * Baby-sitters
* Day-care workers

1,914. Laugh at your child's jokes.

1,915. Let your child know that your truly do enjoy her company.

1,916. Be young-hearted.

1,917. Host a theme picnic for your child in your backyard, like
* French—yummy bread, cheese, and juice
* Junk food—anything goes
* All-American—hot dogs and hamburgers
* Dessert only—yummy treats

1,918. Set off fireworks on
* Birthdays   * Anniversaries
* Special celebrations

1,919. Be a good listener for your child, by
* Not lecturing   * Asking good questions
* Paying attention   * Not interrupting

1,920. Set up a trust fund for your child.

1,921. Keep a journal of your most special times with your child and give it to her on an important birthday.

1,922. Send more than one greeting card to your child, for
  * Birthdays   * Valentine's Day
  * Christmas   * Get well

1,923. Fix hot cocoa and oatmeal on cold mornings.

1,924. Make sure that your child remembers
  * Grandparents' birthdays
  * Your mate's birthday
  * Siblings' birthdays
  * Friend's birthdays
  * Pet's birthday

1,925. Play with your child's toys and allow yourself to have a wonderfully good time.

————————— ♥ —————————

A new commandment I give unto you,
that you love one another.

John 13:34

————————— ♥ —————————

1,926. When you leave your child with a sitter, be
sure to provide a way for the sitter to
entertain your child.

1,927. On Halloween, give a reward to the family
member for the best
* Costume   * Scary story
* Collection of candy

1,928. Order an enormous submarine sandwich
for lunch for just you and your child.

1,929. When your child is doing a big chore, stop
him in the middle of it for a big hug.

1,930. Teach your child that she is
     * Capable   * Lovable
     * Good   * Important
     * Worthwhile

1,931. Buy a Polaroid camera to capture fun times with your child instantly.

1,932. Host a family-member-of-the-month award banquet for the entire clan.

1,933. Greet your child with a gigantic smile.

1,934. Teach your child the art of self-motivation.

1,935. Memorize your child's favorite poem.

1,936. When you go to the bakery for breakfast rolls, be sure to buy some cookies for your child's afternoon snack.

1,937. Take your child to see the changing of the guard at Buckingham Palace and bring poetry to life.

1,938. Start a garden of family heirloom plants.

1,939. Teach your child that he is never too old to learn something new that is of interest to him whether it is a skill, subject, or talent.

1,940. Take a year off from work and spend it with your child.

1,941. Teach your child that there are times to pray
    * On bended knee   * With head bowed
    * Hands folded

1,942. Teach your child that there are other times when a whispered prayer is more appropriate.

1,943. Teach your child that anytime is right for prayer.

1,944. Have your parents tell your children about the good old days.

1,945. Make eye contact with your child when you talk to her.

1,946. Let your child bring along a friend when you have errands to run.

I talk and talk and talk, and I haven't taught people in fifty years what my father taught by example in one week.

Mario Cuomo

1,947. Teach your child to strive for excellence.

1,948. View your child as a masterpiece in progress.

1,949. Buy educational software for your home computer and let your child have fun while learning.

1,950. Change your child's toothbrush every three months.

1,951. Have your child wear bug repellent, long pants, and a long-sleeve shirt when he plays outside at night.

1,952. Leave your work behind at the office when you take a family trip.

1,953. Have realistic expectations about
    * Family vacations
    * Family holiday gatherings

1,954. Keep in mind that family vacations are precious. Many families never even get to take one. Make memories to last a lifetime!

1,955. Make your child "boss for the day," on Boss's Day on October 16.

1,956. Get to know your child's
    * Dentist   * Doctor
    * Tutor   * Principal

1,957. Write a congratulatory letter for special achievements.

1,958. Create a wall of family photos that show warm, loving times.

PARENTING QUESTIONS TO ASK YOURSELF

* Is my child proud of me?
* Do I parent like my mother or my dad? Is that good or bad?
* Do I force my dreams on my child?
* How much time do I spend with my child when we just enjoy each other's company?

1,959. Encourage aunts, uncles, and grandparents to praise your child for her achievements and good behavior, but most important for being a wonderful human being.

1,960. Make sure that all family members thoroughly understand the house rules.

1,961. Let your child choose his own reward for a special achievement.

1,962. Teach your child to celebrate
* Himself   * Life
* Religion   * Small victories
* Loved ones   * Animal friendships
* Achievements

1,963. Know when to leave your child alone so that she can sort out her feelings.

1,964. Take a backward walk with your child.

1,965. Understand that you are God's gift to your child.

1,966. Have a family "show and tell" session at least once a month. You will learn what is important or interesting to your child.

1,967. Teach your child the power of
* Faith   * Visualization
* Dreams   * Imagination

1,968. Teach your child that she is bigger than her fears.

1,969. Understand that your child is a gift from God to you.

1,970. Frame your child's artwork and hang it in the living room.

1,971. Always honor your child.

1,972. Expect your child to bring more joy than sorrow.

1,973. Never have a child to repair a shaky marriage.

1,974. Choose a good pediatrician by
    * Checking his credentials
    * Checking how he handles emergencies
    * Finding out about his billing practices
    * Determining if he honors your insurance
    * Asking if he can be reached at all times in an emergency

1,975. Never let your child hear you say that you are glad that he is
* Going back to school
* Going away to camp
* Visiting out-of-town relatives
He needs to feel that you always want him around!

1,976. Remember the names of your child's
* Teachers   * Friends
* Classmates

1,977. Participate in marches for a worthy cause with your child.

1,978. Show your child that there are many ways of looking at the world.

Happy families are all alike;
every unhappy family is unhappy
in its own way.

Leo Tolstoy

1,979. Keep inspirational books, tapes, and magazines in your home.

1,980. Write a book with your child.

1,981. Dedicate your book to your child.

1,982. Never hide a spare key to your home outside for your child to find because burglars might find it.

1,983. Expand your child's world in little ways, like
* New activities
* Different playgrounds
* Off-beat stores
* Out of the way restaurants
* Unusual toys
* Trendy books

1,984. Make lunchtime sandwiches more fun by using
* Bagels   * Rolls
* Pitas   * Different flavors of bread

1,985. Instead of waiting for a party, play old-fashioned party games with your family, like:
* Blindman's Buff
* London Bridge
* Musical Chairs
* Murder
* Charades

1,986. Pave the way for your child to become a great parent by one day by setting an example of a model parent.

1,987. Never label your child in an unflattering manner.

1,988. Make a homemade movie of you and your mate sharing your feelings of love for your child.

1,989. Discuss with your child how you two can help children in other parts of the world.

1,990. Leave a trail of candy for your child to follow to find you or a special gift.

1,991. When you give clothing as a gift, consider
    * Your child's current wardrobe
    * Your child's taste
    * Your child's needs
    * Your child's size and body type

1,992. Keep in mind that your child sees the world differently than you do.

1,993. Look for the innocence in your child.

1,994. Take your child to one of the many events held at large bookstores, like:
    * Book signings   * Lectures
    * Concerts   * Book clubs

1,995. Frame travel posters from wonderful family vacations for your child's room.

1,996. Be careful when you and your mate argue and explain to your child that it isn't his fault when you and your spouse disagree.

1,997. Consider being a foster family and giving another child or children the benefit and blessing of your family.

1,998. Keep in mind that you have many roles, like
   * Friend   * Employee
   * Neighbor   * Sibling
   * Daughter/Son
   Your role as a parent is the most important!

1,999. If you have had a foreign exchange student live with your family, take your child to visit his homeland.

2,000. Inspire your child to dare to undertake great things.

2,001. Ask your child to give you a list of things that will make him feel loved.

2,002. Before she goes to bed at night, remind her of something good that she did today or that happened in her life.

---------♥---------

I looked on child rearing not only
as a work of love and duty but as
a profession that was fully interesting
and challenging as any honorable
profession in the world and one that
demanded the best that I could
bring to it.

Rose Kennedy

---------♥---------

ABOUT THE AUTHOR

Cyndi Haynes is the best-selling author of seven books in the 2,002 series, including 2,002 Ways to Cheer Yourself Up. Her books have been published in twelve languages. To promote her books she has appeared on hundreds of radio and television programs, including Ricki Lake and Gordon Elliott. Her books have been written about in numberous publications, including Glamour, Redbook, and Cosmopolitan. She lives in Indiana with her husband, son, two golden retrievers, and a Bernese mountain dog.